LIVE IT. BE IT.

LIVING AS GOD CREATED YOU TO BE

BENTON J. WARD

COPYRIGHT

For my mother, Anita, brother and sister, Joel and Danielle, my wife Megan, and all those who have been such a huge part of my journey: Joanna, Pastor Anthony, Pastor Darren, TJ, and all others that I don't have room to mention. Thank you all for the hours listening to me rant, for providing advice and wisdom, and for challenging and encouraging me to be the best I can be. I would not be where I am without you. I love you all.

TABLE OF CONTENTS

INTRODUCTION

Have you ever felt stuck in your spiritual life? It may seem like you can't hear God's voice. Maybe it feels like you don't know what to believe anymore. That nothing you are being taught is adding up. You might also be dealing with various levels of frustration, maybe even depression. Are you going in circles trying to ease these feelings? Here's some encouraging news. You're not alone. It happens to all of us in various stages of our walk with Jesus. I believe the biggest reason we experience these emotions is because God is trying to change things up in our lives and either we aren't aware of it or we are unwilling to make the necessary changes to experience what He wants to do in our lives. I've experienced this several times, especially in the past few years.

There have been dreams that God has given me throughout the years. Some I have achieved. Others I didn't pursue. Without realizing it, I neglected the gifts and talents that God had given to me in order to accomplish other goals that I thought were God-given opportunities. In reality, they were other people's dreams that I liked. Trying to find my place in life, I committed to those different ministry opportunities, taking on the tasks myself to help others fulfill their dreams. What I didn't realize was, they weren't God's will for me. Committing to them without waiting for God to confirm that it was His plan was a mistake. This led to a lot of emotional pain and spiritual frustration.

For years, I felt like I was going around in circles. I could never seem to find peace about the decisions I was making. I thought that maybe I just needed to grow more. So, I read books and listened to podcasts. I prayed and fasted. Yet nothing seemed to help. I kept thinking, if I can just push through this sense of wrongness, I can find peace. Even though I've always been a joyful person, my emotional health spiraled, causing my spiritual life to spiral as well. I've never experienced depression, but during this time I came close to it. I noticed myself becoming more and more frustrated with everything. As I was experiencing this, I lost motivation to continue in ministry. I became burnt out and afraid I would just continue to make the same mistakes again.

At the time this was happening, I was volunteering as the young adults pastor of my church in Louisville, Ky. With the help of my pastor and a friend who was a life coach, and a lot of self-examination and prayer, I gained an awareness of what was happening inside of me. I was doing too much. I wasn't being who God wanted me to be. I had neglected my giftings and stopped pursuing dreams God had put inside of me in order to do things I was not called to do.

After realizing this, God challenged me to follow Him and let Him lead me into a new season of growth. He told me to give up my position as young adult pastor so that He could do something new in my life. I resigned and since then, God has led me on a unique and challenging journey I didn't expect. A journey where He has taught me to be His follower and let Him lead me to where He wants me and make me like Him.

DOING VERSUS BEING

As I've walked with Him on this journey, there is something God has shown me. The reason many people's dreams die is that they have a DO mentality instead of a BE mentality. This is also the reason they become burnt out and give up. Let me explain what I mean by this by using my story as an example.

Spending so much time DOING ministry caused me to lose focus on BEING a follower of Jesus. I didn't sin, have a moral failure, and I never got to where I suffered from severe depression. I did, however, DO so much that it distracted me from being who I was supposed to BE. It wasn't my responsibility to DO the work of a pastor. It was to BE a follower of Jesus who surrendered my pastoral giftings to Him and let Him grow people through me. I also neglected my giftings, and as a result, I was never complete and whole in Him.

Just like me, the Church has been doing a lot. We DO things like go to war or build governments in the name of Christ. Some DO things like preach against abortion, same sex marriage, sex before marriage, or whatever conservative political/moral stance we take as Christians. We DO missionary work or give to charities to say we are sharing God's love with people. Christians go to church where we sing, hear sermons about living right, doing more for Jesus, etc. We hang out with our Christian friends. We listen to Christian music. A lot of Christians complain about how corrupt society is. None of these things are bad. However, the motives and mindsets we have can be problematic. Especially if our mindset is that we need to DO things in order to "be good Christians."

Having a DO mentality dooms us to fail. When we DO things to be "good Christians", we operate from our own understanding and our own power, instead of God's. Even if we have the best intentions, it will cause us to fail. We hear of leadership burnout, suicide, moral failure, religious legalism, heretical beliefs, stagnation, and complacency in the church. Churches are dying or falling into heresy. I believe this is because we've focused on DOING "churchy" things and have forgotten how to BE like Christ to the community.

Learning how to BE instead of DO teaches us to BE like Him. As we BE His followers, we let Him do what He wants to do. Being takes the pressure off of us having to do things to grow and puts it on God Himself to build His own church. We don't have to DO anything other than BE His followers. Yes, as we follow Him, we will do things as He leads. However, it will be in His power, not ours. The things that He wants us to do aren't a requirement. They won't change our relationship with Him other than to help us grow. They are a privilege. A way to enjoy life following Him while bringing others along. They are also ways for us to represent Him well on the earth. As we follow Him, He does the work through us to grow His kingdom.

People need to see Jesus. Our responsibility is to live out the gospel and BE the light that we are called to be. That can only happen if we stop trying to DO things that don't matter and start learning what it means to BE His disciples.

I hope that as you read this book, you will embark on this journey as well. Learn to BE His follower and BE like Him. Let's do it together.

CHAPTER 1
KNOWING GOD

Am I a believer or a follower of Jesus? Every person who calls themselves a Christian should ask themselves this question. What is the difference between a believer in Jesus and a follower of Jesus? The Bible gives the best answer in James 2: 14-20.

> *"What does it profit, my brethren, if someone says he*
> *has faith but does not have works? Can faith*
> *save him? If a brother or sister is naked and*
> *destitute of daily food, and one of you says to*
> *them, 'Depart in peace, be warmed and filled,'*
> *but you do not give them the things which are*
> *needed for the body, what does it profit? Thus*
> *also faith by itself, if it does not have works, is*
> *dead. But someone will say, 'You have faith, and*
> *I have works.' Show me your faith without your*
> *works, and I will show you my faith by my works.*
> *You believe that there is one God. You do well.*
> *Even the demons believe—and tremble! But do*

you want to know, O foolish man, that faith
without works is dead?"

FAITH THAT'S ALIVE

What is the difference between a believer and a follower of Jesus? I'll put it simply. A believer is someone who believes in God. A follower of Jesus follows Him. Before I go any further, though, let me say one thing to explain myself. I don't want you to think I'm speaking blasphemy. I am not saying that those who call themselves "believers" are not true Christians. The Bible makes it very clear in Romans 10:9 that those who believe in their hearts and confess with their mouths that Jesus is Lord are saved. I am, however, clarifying the differences between someone who just has a general belief in God versus someone who has given their life to follow Jesus.

"Believers" have a basic knowledge of biblical teaching, but don't follow the way of Jesus. Their faith is dead. They don't put what they say they believe into action. In fact, they follow the example of the demons who believe in Jesus and tremble before Him, but do not follow Him. Some keep people from following Him by deceiving them and keeping them blind to the truth. As a result, they are kept bound to sin and death. Jesus says this about them in Matthew 7: 21-23.

> *"Not everyone who says to Me, 'Lord, Lord,' shall*
> *enter the kingdom of heaven, but he who does the*
> *will of My Father in heaven. Many will say to Me*
> *in that day, 'Lord, Lord, have we not prophesied*
> *in Your name, cast out demons in Your name, and*
> *done many wonders in Your name?' And then I*
> *will declare to them, 'I never knew you; depart*
> *from Me, you who practice lawlessness!'*

People who believe in Him but don't follow Him don't truly know Him and He doesn't know them.

A follower of Jesus, however, loves Him and follows His teachings. They live their lives experiencing Him and following Him in obedience. Some even follow Him to their deaths. Their faith is alive and well. Jesus Himself, in John 10, describes His followers as sheep who know His voice. Because they love and trust Him, they follow His voice with everything they are and have, never being led astray by another.

KNOWING ABOUT OR KNOWING

Being aware of where we are on our journey with Jesus is very important. We need to ask ourselves a very important question. "Do I know about Jesus or do I know Him?" The only way to answer this is to examine your lifestyle. What do you do to grow your relationship with Jesus? How much time do you spend with Him, learning who He is? How much do you read Scripture or spend time in prayer? These two practices are essential to learning who He is and developing our relationships with Him.

Through studying the Bible, we develop an understanding of God's character. We also learn to BE like Him as we follow Him in obedience and faith. Through prayer, or communicating with God, He reveals Himself to us and opens our eyes to the truth. Scripture comes alive at this moment. As a result, we are forever changed. Our relationship with Him deepens as we continue to experience His presence and develop healthy communication habits with Him.

Communication is a two-way process between two individuals. When we pray, not only are we communicating to God through our prayers; He is communicating back to us. When we communicate with someone every day, that person becomes more than just an acquaintance. We learn who they are and a relationship is formed. For the relationship to thrive, there must be consistent, intentional, healthy communication. Our relationship with God works the same way. We must have consistent, healthy times of intentional communication with God through prayer.

Let me give three examples to emphasize what I am saying.

- *ACCESS TO RELATIONSHIP*

George Washington was the first President of the United States. History books teach us a lot about who he was. However, I can't know George Washington because he's dead. It's impossible to communicate and develop a relationship with him. We have a lot of information about him in the history books that gives some knowledge about him. However, even with this knowledge, we cannot know everything about him. Because he is dead, we do not have access to him. We only have the limited information provided in history books about his accomplishments.

Jesus, however, is not just a person in the history books. He rose from the grave over 2000 years ago. While He Himself is not here, He sent His Holy Spirit to help us BE like Him as we follow Him. He is with us and never leaves. We have a level of access to Him we have with no one else. We can take advantage of this access if we want a relationship with Him. As we seek Him with our whole hearts, He speaks to us and reveals Himself.

- *OPINIONS VERSUS TRUTH*

My next example is the former President of the United States, Donald Trump. I know about Donald Trump, or at least what the media tells me. However, this knowledge is limited and could be incorrect. Until I develop a relationship with him, I will never know who he is. Another point is this. How we view someone is influenced by what we are told or how we feel. We've heard all kinds of things about President Trump that might have influenced our perception of him. Some might have been true, some false. Some love him more, some hate him more, regardless of the truth of what was said.

The same applies to our relationship with God. I can gain knowledge about God by several means, including reading the Bible or listening to what people say about Him. However, until I develop a relationship with Him through healthy prayer and intentional study, I will never truly know God. Unfortunately, even those who claim to know God today don't actually know Him.

According to studies by the Barna Group and other researchers who study religious trends, over 60% of those who claim to be Christians do not know what the Bible actually says. Because they don't read the bible, the average American Christian only knows God based on what others have told them. This means that Christians in our society today don't know the voice of God. They can be led astray by false teachings and their own emotions telling them how to live their lives. God is communicating, but they aren't listening. Paul puts it like this in 2 Timothy 4:3-4.

> *"For the time will come when they will not endure*
> *sound doctrine, but according to their own*
> *desires, because they have itching ears, they will*
> *heap up for themselves teachers; and they will*
> *turn their ears away from the truth, and be*
> *turned aside to fables."*

Let me give you an example that may shock some of you. We have been taught since we were kids in church that Noah took two of each kind of animal, male and female, into the ark. This isn't what the Bible says. Look it up for yourself if you don't believe me. In Genesis 7, God commanded Noah to take seven clean animals, seven birds, and two unclean animals, male and female of each kind, on the ark. I have been reading and hearing the Bible since I was four years old. I did not realize that this is what it said until I was twenty-four. For twenty years, I believed what people were teaching. While that might not seem important, it's scary to think about the fact that there might be other things we're hearing taught in church that are incorrect.

Here's another cultural example. During Christmas, we see the Nativity Scene put on display everywhere. It's such an excellent reminder that Jesus is the "reason for the season," as people used to say. It shows the shepherds, wise men, Mary, Joseph, the sheep all celebrating around the manger with Baby Jesus in it. This is wonderful imagery that sparks a sense of joy and hope. There's a problem, though. The Nativity Scene is not biblically accurate. The wise men weren't at Jesus' birth. They came from the east at least eighteen months afterwards. For years, this scene has shown an inaccurate portrayal of this story. No one has ever corrected it. Again, just like the ark reference, this might not seem that important. However, it sparks the question. What else are we learning that is inaccurate?

Please, please, please hear me when I say that we need to study the Bible and not just trust what people are saying about God. This is the only way for us to BE like Him. We have to know Him and what He says to follow Him well.

- *RELATIONSHIP TAKES EFFORT*

Here's another way to put it. How many of you have problems making friends? Maybe you're an introvert. Maybe you feel like nobody wants to hang out with you? How many of you intentionally avoid people? My point is you will not have many friends if you aren't intentional about making friendships. We can also look at this in a romantic context. We all know people who are single. Some of you might be in that stage of life. Here's the thing, though. If you don't put yourself out there to find someone, you'll stay single forever. The same can be said of our relationship with God. You must seek Him with your whole heart if you want to find Him. Then, when you find Him, the next step is to develop a relationship with Him.

If you are dating someone, the relationship will never grow past the honeymoon phase if you don't get to know one another. Relationships are also a two-way street. It takes both parties being intentional to create a relationship. Both must engage in healthy, consistent communication. Otherwise, you're wasting your time.

Now, while I know our relationship with God is not a romantic relationship, the same principle illustrated in these examples still applies. In order to grow a relationship with God, you must spend quality time with Him communicating.

Something else I want to point out about relationships is that they help you grow. The Bible says that iron sharpens iron. This illustrates that relationships sharpen you as a person. God wants to have this kind of relationship with us. He wants to sharpen us as we walk with Him so we can BE more like Him.

TRANSFORMING RELATIONSHIP

You might ask, what does this chapter have to do with me? I already have a good relationship with Jesus. I'm already a good Christian person, so how does it help me be a better Christian? I want to answer this question by using a part of my story as an example.

Growing up in a Christian home, I had heard about Jesus my whole life and knew how to live a "Christian" life. However, having a knowledge of God means nothing unless you experience Him for yourself. Once you do, you will fall in love with Him and BE more like Him. This growth can only happen as you build a relationship with Him. Also, as you follow Him, you have to allow Him to work on you, changing you from the inside out. This is the only way for you to BE like Him and BE who He has called you to BE. For me, the result of experiencing His presence and following Him was an entire personality change.

When I was growing up, I was extremely shy. I was always a nervous wreck, stuttering when I spoke to people. Making new friends was hard. Then, when I was fifteen years old, I had an encounter with God while at youth camp. He called me into ministry, telling me that I was going to be a worship leader for young adults. You can imagine the confusion I felt upon hearing this. I didn't play an instrument or sing and was still struggling severely with insecurities. It also made little sense why He had said young adults. I wasn't a young adult yet. I was fifteen. All I knew, though, was that God had spoken to me and revealed my calling. This experience led to transformation and put me on the path leading to where I am today.

From the time I was fifteen years old up to this point as an adult, God has completely changed me. I went from being an extremely shy, insecure teenager to being a "flaming extrovert" as a good friend once called me. A loud, joyful, confident person who can talk to anyone about anything. He changed my entire personality over the years through the empowerment of the Holy Spirit, allowing me to accomplish the purpose He had for me.

The point of this personal testimony is this. It's not enough to know about God. I could have decided the values instilled by my parents were enough to get me by. What would have happened to me if I had just relied on my knowledge of God instead of seeking Him and going deeper? I would not have not experienced the transformation that I needed to become who I am today.

I have been leading worship for young adults since I was in college, fulfilling the original calling God gave me as a fifteen year old at that youth camp. It didn't stop there, though. As I've walked with Him, God has expanded that calling. He has opened up doors for me to not only be a worship leader, but also a pastor, a missionary, and now a writer. He has transformed me, and equipped me to fulfill the purpose He has for me. Where before I couldn't speak to anyone, especially in front of people, I can now lead worship and preach in front of thousands if given the opportunity. None of this would have happened if I only knew about God. Instead, I have walked with Jesus, developing a healthy, thriving relationship with Him. He transformed me and is still transforming me. I'm no longer who I was even a year ago. Yes, I am still growing and have a lot to learn, but I'm growing with Him beside me. He wants to do the same thing in you as well. All it takes is for us to say "yes" when He calls us to follow Him. Yes, it does take sacrifice, but it is worth it.

BE WITH JESUS

The perfect example of transformation found in the Bible is Peter. In Acts 4, Peter and John had been preaching at the temple in Jerusalem. The religious leaders did not like this, but were astonished by their boldness and knowledge of scripture. They recognized they had been with Jesus.

Spending time with Jesus had transformed the disciples and equipped them to go beyond their natural capabilities. Peter was the perfect demonstration of this. Only weeks before the Day of Pentecost, he had denied that he knew Jesus three times. Even though he had spent three years following Him, he still needed more transformation to overcome his fear. Then something happened inside of him that pushed him to grow beyond this weakness. After His resurrection, He experienced Jesus in a way he never had before. This experience broke the fear he had and changed him, giving him what he needed to decide never to live in fear again. On the Day of Pentecost, he stood up boldly and preached about Jesus to thousands of people. Three thousand started following Jesus that day, and thousands were added to the church after that. This would not have happened if Peter had not allowed his relationship with Jesus to transform him.

I want to point out something in this verse. Peter showed not only that he knew Jesus, but that he also knew scripture that backed up what he was saying about Jesus. He preached to the people and their eyes were opened to the truth. This shows us that studying scripture is essential to finding out who Jesus is. As we study, the Holy Spirit deepens our understanding of scripture and our relationship with God. Once that happens, scripture becomes alive and real to us. We understand that it's all about Jesus and we experience Him in deeper ways that help us on our journey to BE like Him.

FALSE TEACHINGS

Studying scripture helps us to have a healthy understanding of God. Lacking a healthy understanding of scripture partnered with a healthy lifestyle of communicating with God causes us to have a distorted view of who God is. Throughout the history of the church, there have been a lot of distorted views of God and twisted opinions of scripture. These distortions have influenced Christians in every denomination. They are the reason there is such a lack of biblical literacy and a rise of false doctrines in the modern Church. Before I go any further in this book, I want to address two of these false views of God that have kept Christians from understanding and living out the will of God.

- *HAPPY VERSUS HOLY*

The first one that I believe has caused the most damage to the church is the idea that God wants you to "be happy" and to "follow your heart". This view has caused the people of God to follow their emotions instead of the Holy Spirit. It is not a scriptural concept and can give Christians the idea that it is ok to live lifestyles that are not pleasing to God. Scripture makes it very plain in Galatians that God does not want us to follow our emotions. He wants us to follow the leading of the Holy Spirit.

Our emotions are corrupted by our sinful natures, and can be changed in an instant by situations and struggles. The enemy knows this and knows how to use our emotions to lead us astray if we aren't careful. Therefore, doing what "makes us happy" isn't always wise.

When we are led by the Holy Spirit instead of our emotions, we allow His character to manifest in our lives. Paul talks about this in Galatians 5 when he teaches about the fruit of the Spirit: love, joy, peace, patience, kindness, goodness, faithfulness, gentleness, and self-control. While each fruit can cause feelings such as happiness, they are not emotions. They are lifestyles every Christian should have if they are following the Holy Spirit. Unlike emotions, these lifestyles cannot be changed by situation or trials. This means that even though we might be sad, we still have joy. We might be angry, but still love. We might have desires, but we operate in self-control. Even if it's hard and we might not want to, we still choose to not rely only on our emotions and desire for happiness. We rely on the Holy Spirit. This is very important, especially in discerning God's will. God can speak to us in feelings, but will always confirm those feelings with other things. It's always better to wait until we have those confirmations before we jump into something because our emotions tell us to. Christ was the perfect example of someone who didn't follow His emotions but instead walked in the Spirit. Our goal is to BE like Him. We must choose every day to surrender our emotions to Him and let the Holy Spirit renew and strengthen us.

- *ANGRY, FIRE AND BRIMSTONE GOD*

There is another false view of God that has created chaos in the church for hundreds of years. It is the teaching that God is an angry God who sends lightning and fire to strike down those who disobey Him. This teaching says we have to try to live perfect lives, never messing up or He will strike us down. However, this view contradicts what scripture says in Ephesians: it's by grace that we have been saved, through faith, not by works. It also takes away from the purpose of the cross. Our actions don't determine our salvation. Jesus paid the price so we don't have to DO anything. All we have to do is to BE His followers. Yes, scripture is very clear that God wants us to obey Him and that there will be punishment for those who don't follow Him. However, scripture is also very clear that there is no way that we can be perfect on our own. We need help. God made it clear through the law that there had to be a sacrifice of a perfect, spotless lamb each year in order for their sins to be forgiven. Jesus was our perfect, spotless lamb. His sacrifice on the cross covered our sins, past, present, and future, when we follow Him. This means that those of us who love and follow Jesus never have to worry. Our current struggles and sins will not disqualify us from being saved. Our sins have already been forgiven. The goal now is to allow the Holy Spirit to transform us into who God desires us to BE.

If this is true, this teaching doesn't add up. Why would God send fire down to punish us? We're always going to mess up. If He sent fire every time we messed up, none of us would be here. Even followers of Jesus would be struck down by His judgment and wrath because we still mess up. This mentality keeps us in a state of fear and can keep us from doing God's will. We will fear messing up so much that we don't actually do what He's called us to do. When discerning His will for our lives, it is important to remember that even though God wants us to be perfect, we will never be one hundred percent perfect. The good thing is, God doesn't use perfect people. All throughout scripture we see that He uses messed up people who have lots of issues. In fact, it's the best way for His glory to be shown. His strength and glory will be shown in our weaknesses. That's His promise, and He proves this time and time again. This takes a lot of the pressure off of us to be perfect. However, this does not give us permission to do whatever we want. God gave us a way to BE like Him with the help of the Holy Spirit. We have to choose to do things His way instead of our own, though. His power takes us as we are and transforms us into the people He wants us to BE. He makes us like Christ and equips us for the purpose He has called us to.

DISCERNMENT

I believe it is very important for us as Christians to be aware of false views of God. Another more "churchy" word for this awareness is spiritual discernment or knowing what is truth or not. These teachings limit us from becoming who God has called us to be. Jesus said that the church that He was building would be a church that the gates of hell could not stand against. This cannot happen if we, as Christians, do not know the truth. We can't follow the God we say we serve if we don't know the difference between the truth and a lie. The pastor of the church I went to in college had this saying:

"Crucify your opinion and let the Bible speak for itself." We need to study the Bible while crucifying our opinions so we can know what God is saying and then obey. This is the only way to know and follow Him and BE like Him. Saying we believe is one thing. Doing it is another. Take up your cross and follow Jesus.

THE CHALLENGE

I want to emphasize again that following Jesus requires a lifestyle of studying scripture partnered with a lifestyle of active communication with the Holy Spirit through prayer. The Holy Spirit opens our eyes to the truth of who Jesus is and then He empowers us to obey so we can BE more like Him. It requires humility to say I need more of Him. We then have to choose each day to crucify our opinions and feelings in order to study scripture. We must submit to the Holy Spirit's leading and let Him reveal the truth to us, even when that truth might be just how wrong we are and how much we need to repent and change. The good thing is that truth partnered with the power of the Holy Spirit can set us free. We are then given the opportunity to move forward in our lives with Him, growing to BE like Him.

Another challenging thought I want to end with is this. There are people in your life who look up to you. They are depending on you to be Jesus to them. If you aren't developing your relationship with Him in a way that transforms you, then you are doing yourself and the surrounding people a disservice. You aren't living and bringing glory to God the way He wants you to. The most important step in your walk with God is to go beyond just knowing about God, to truly knowing Him in a way that transforms you and those around you.

CHAPTER 2
MY WILL, HIS WILL

"Not my will but yours be done."

T hese words echo through my mind as I write this next chapter. "Not my will, but Yours be done." Jesus, the Son of God. The Messiah. The one destined to be the Savior of the world put His wants and desires away so that the Father could see His plan accomplished on the earth.

We see Jesus going through a lot of suffering in the following chapters of the Gospels. We see Him endure mockery, whippings, and ultimately, His death on the cross. That isn't all we see, though. We also see His triumphant resurrection, ascension into heaven, and the ultimate birth of the Church on the day of Pentecost. These events occurred because He gave up His will. He put aside his fear of pain, in order to achieve the Father's greater plan that would lead to the best results. He put His desires aside so that the punishment for our sins could be fully paid and we could be brought back into a relationship with God.

So how can we take what we see in this account and apply it to our lives as followers of Jesus? How do we recognize God's will and put aside our own wills to achieve His?

MY WILL VS GOD'S WILL

Have you ever had an opportunity that you thought was the will of God but it wasn't? It probably started out pretty great. Maybe it turned around and fell apart, though. Most of us who follow Jesus can say "been there, done that." Some of us learn from those times. Some of us don't, making the same mistakes repeatedly. My friends, I want to tell you a secret. If it falls apart, it probably wasn't God's will. Or it was and most likely your will got in the way and you did the right thing the wrong way, causing it to fall apart. Fortunately, God's plan and ways include grace and restoration. If you got off of the path that He set you on, He is faithful to forgive and set you back on course. He loves to restore what you broke and make it better. He can't do this, though, until we choose to repent and do things His way.

So, how do we recognize our will versus God's? To answer this question, I want to talk about two things for the rest of this chapter. First, I want to spend some time discussing what the Bible says about the flesh. We, as humans, must realize we are at war with our flesh. Especially those of us who claim to follow Jesus. Second, I want to talk about how our personality types play a part in how we make choices, good or bad. We all have strengths and weaknesses that come with our personality types. We must learn how to surrender these to God and let Him change us.

THE FLESH AND THE SPIRIT

According to the Bible in Genesis chapter 1, when man was first created, God created him in His own image and then breathed life into him. God is a spirit, though. He does not have a physical body. So what this means is that God created man with all of His characteristics. He created man with the ability to feel emotions and to think rationally in order to make conscious decisions. This separates us from animals who operate on instinct and emotion alone. God created Adam for relationship as well, first with Himself and then with Eve too. This also separates us from animals. When God breathed His breath into Adam, His Spirit entered Him, giving Him life and power. The Spirit enabled him to live out the calling that God created him to have. Because God is a perfect person who is completely good, Adam inherited His goodness as well.

Wanting us to have free will, God gave Adam and Eve a choice. He commanded them not to eat the fruit of the knowledge of good and evil. He wanted them to remain pure, never knowing about evil. However, He also loved them enough to give them a choice. We find out in this story that Adam and Eve both disobeyed this command, choosing evil. As a result, sin and death entered the world, corrupting the entire universe from that moment on. Without realizing it, Adam and Eve gave up the characteristics of God, including His goodness, and became corrupted by evil. For humanity, this corruption became known as the flesh. This is our natural tendency to choose our own corrupt desires which lead us away from His plan for our lives. This leads to separation from God. Evil and death cannot exist in His presence.

Fortunately, God's plan to redeem humanity and bring us back into a relationship included a gift: the Holy Spirit. Scripture says that it is the Holy Spirit who "convicts the world of sin" in John 16:8. He also reveals the truth about Jesus and glorifies Him in John 16:13-14. He then transforms us by renewing and sanctifying our minds in Romans 12:2. When we listen to and obey the Holy Spirit, we become His temple, according to 1 Corinthians 6:19-20. This is when He starts to make us like Him again.

Even with the Spirit's renewing, our flesh is still there. However, just because it's a part of us does not mean that it has control over us. We choose to give it control. The key to overcoming our fleshly tendencies is to be aware of them. Then, when temptation comes, we have to listen to the Holy Spirit as He speaks and helps us resist our flesh.

So how do we recognize our fleshly tendencies? Well, my answer to that question is that our fleshly tendencies and habits are the opposite of the character of God. Paul gives us examples of the behaviors of those who are controlled by their flesh in Galatians 5. He also gives the fruit of the Spirit, or characteristics of God, that each follower of Jesus should produce in their lives. Let's look at the examples of fleshly behavior first: adultery, sorcery, hatred, contentions, jealousies, outbursts of wrath, selfish ambitions, dissensions, heresies, envy, murders, drunkenness, revelries, etc. Now let's look at the fruit of the Spirit he mentions: love, joy, peace, patience, kindness, goodness, faithfulness, gentleness, and self-control. I mentioned these in my last chapter.

- *Fruit of the Spirit*

As I mentioned above, one of the Holy Spirit's roles in our lives is to transform and renew our minds. This can only happen when we listen and submit to His leading. I mentioned in the last chapter that the fruit we produce comes from spending time with Him. As we develop our relationship with Him and listen to His Spirit, He reveals our fleshly tendencies He wants to change. Once we realize them, we have to allow Him to teach us how to resist. This is the only way He can transform us to be more like Him. The behaviors of our flesh are the opposite of the character of God. In fact, we see by the examples listed by Paul in Galatians that our fleshly tendency and nature are the absence of God's spirit working in our lives. God's spirit is absent until we choose to give our lives to Him. He also can't work in our lives when we choose to ignore Him in moments of temptation.

We must have a relationship with the Spirit so we can learn to BE like Jesus. For instance, if we are to emulate and produce the fruit of love, we have to first have a relationship with the One who is and has perfect love. The absence of His love in our lives results in selfish ambitions, dissensions, jealousies, murders, and all of those other fleshly behaviors that cause division in our lives.

The same thing applies to the other fruit. When we aren't faithful to the One who is Truth made flesh, the absence of that truth in our lives will lead to our destruction. We will believe lies and false teachings instead of the truth that sets us free. I mentioned some of these lies in the last chapter. When we aren't faithful to our spouses, the absence of that love and commitment to honoring them will lead to adultery. If we aren't experiencing the patience, gentleness, and kindness of Jesus, the absence of these traits will produce violence, murder, dissensions, and ultimately, our destruction. When we aren't actively listening to the conviction of the Holy Spirit, we won't use self-control. Our lives will be filled with drunkenness and revelries that will bring destruction as well. The list goes on.

- *Temptation*

Even for a follower of Jesus, the flesh can impede us from living fully in the will of God. Because of our sin nature, our flesh will always come between us and a life of complete perfection and wholeness. Paul puts it this way in Romans 7:14-20.

> *"For we know that the law is spiritual, but I am*
> *carnal, sold under sin. For what I am doing, I do*
> *not understand. For what I will to do, that I do*

not practice; but what I hate, that I do. If, then, I do what I will not to do, I agree with the law that it is good. But now, it is no longer I who do it, but sin that dwells in me. For I know that in me (that is, in my flesh) nothing good dwells; for to will is present with me, but how to perform what is good I do not find. For the good that I will to do, I do not do; but the evil I will not to do, that I practice. Now if I do what I will not to do, it is no longer I who do it, but sin that dwells in me."

Basically, what he is saying here is that sometimes we still do wrong. Our sin nature can still rise in moments of weakness. We don't want to do those things anymore, but still do. We haven't yet learned to have self-control all the time. There are moments where the temptation might seem so strong that it might feel like we have to give in to it in order for it to go away. We want the pleasure of it, even if we know it's not the best for us. Sometimes we might not even know that we're messing up. We learn pretty quickly that it was a mistake, though, when everything falls apart because of our decision. We try to hear God's voice and obey what He tells us, but there will always be moments where the flesh can influence our decisions consciously or unconsciously.

- *Willful Disobedience*

The story of David and Bathsheba in 2 Samuel 12 emphasizes this very well. David had stayed home from a battle and was on his roof looking out over the city. He saw Bathsheba bathing on her roof and immediately desired her. He brought her to the palace to have sex with her. Unfortunately, she became pregnant. Out of fear, guilt and shame, he had her husband murdered in battle so that he could marry her.

In this story, we see a man who followed God to such a degree that he was known in Scripture as the man after God's own heart. He was also the ancestor of Jesus. Even he, as close to God as he was, was tempted and gave in to his own fleshy tendencies. He knew what he was doing was wrong, but did it anyway. The results of giving in to that sinful desire were adultery and murder. It would eventually lead to the death of the son that he and Bathsheba conceived that day. This example shows us that no matter how mature in our faith we are, our flesh is still there. We can still be weak during temptation. We have to learn to combat our flesh in those moments of weakness. The Holy Spirit helps us with this as we learn to listen to His voice convicting and strengthening us during those moments of temptation.

- *Unconscious Disobedience*

There are countless other stories of acts of willful disobedience in the Bible. But what about when we don't know we are messing up?

One way to determine if we are doing God's will or not is to examine the motives behind a decision. We also have to see what the consequences of that decision will be. If our motive is self-serving and wouldn't grow the kingdom or bring God glory, then it is definitely not God's will. If our motive is pure, but the consequences would not be the best for all parties involved, and would bring unwarranted harm to someone else, then it is probably not God's will. It is also most definitely not from God if the decision would cause others to fall into sin or reject God.

God's will occurs in His perfect timing. It will always be for all parties' benefit and His glory. It is always the best plan and will always work out perfectly. To achieve His plan, we follow His instructions, wait on His timing, and do things His way.

There is one story in the Bible that shows this point. In Genesis 12, God had promised Abraham that he would be the father of many nations. He later told him He would give Sarah a son. Unfortunately, Sarah was old and couldn't conceive. When she heard that, she didn't believe it and laughed. She told Abraham to have sex with her servant Hagar in order to give him a son that way. Thinking it was a good idea, Abraham did as Sarah suggested. However, he didn't think about the consequences or consult God about it to see if it was His will or not. Hagar conceived a son that they named Ishmael. Sarah became jealous of Hagar and Ishmael, so she asked Abraham to send them away. God saw Hagar's and Ishmael's trouble, though. He had favor on them and took care of their needs. They made a covenant and Ishmael became the father of several nations.

We see in this story that Abraham and Sarah misinterpreted what God had said. They took matters into their own hands, giving in to their own fleshly tendency of impatience in order to have a son through another means. That wasn't what God had told them, though. He had told them that Sarah would have a son. If they'd have waited a little longer, the son that God had promised them would have been born: Isaac. But, since they didn't wait, it led to conflict and division. We see in the story that despite this division and conflict, God had mercy on them and blessed Ishmael. He became the father of several nations. In fact, we see that several Middle Eastern nations today are direct descendants of Ishmael. Unfortunately, the fruit of the conflict and division created when they kicked them out is still being seen today. The descendants of Ishmael are still in conflict with the descendants of Isaac, Israel. The root of this conflict is jealousy and dissension over who was the son of promise. All of this strife could have been avoided if Abraham and Sarah had not given in to their impatience.

SLAVE TO SIN

Both stories show the need for us to realize our fleshly tendencies and surrender them to God. In the moment of temptation, the fleshly desire might be very strong. However, it's up to us to recognize when our sin nature and flesh is controlling us. We must immediately surrender those desires to the Holy Spirit and allow Him to help us resist temptation. This is the difference between being a slave to sin and a servant of Christ. A slave to sin gives in to fleshly desires and lets those desires control him/her when temptation comes. He/she might feel some shame or regret after committing the sin. However, there is no genuine change or repentance. They continue to sin in the same manner again and again.

In the Bible, King Saul is a perfect illustration of this. He commits the same sin two different times in Scripture and never repents. In 1 Samuel 13, he had been instructed to wait for Samuel to come to sacrifice to God on behalf of the Israelites who were about to go into battle. Saul and the people became impatient and afraid. The Philistines were gathering close by and Samuel had still not come. Instead of waiting longer for Samuel to get there, he disobeyed Samuel and made the sacrifice himself. This was also an act of disobedience against God's command as well. He had established in the law that only the priests could sacrifice for the nation. Saul disobeys a second time in 1 Samuel 15. God had instructed Saul to annihilate the Amalekites and destroy all of their possessions. Saul disobeyed and kept the best of the livestock and wealth. When Samuel confronted him, Saul's response was that he took the best to sacrifice it to the Lord. If this was Saul's intention, this was a noble gesture. But, it was still disobedience to the Lord's command. Saul's unrepentant and disobedient heart cost him the kingdom of Israel. Samuel puts it very well in 1 Samuel 15: 22 with his response that "obedience is better than sacrifice." We must remember this as well that, even though we might have the best intentions, disobedience is never the answer. We must do things His way. If we don't know His way yet, we must seek Him until we find the answer and wait until He tells us.

SERVANT OF CHRIST

A servant of Christ might sin, but repents when they are convicted by the Holy Spirit. Repentance, in the ancient Greek, is the word *metanoia*. This word means to have a mindset change. It implies that when someone truly repents; they have a strong conviction that the sin is wrong. This conviction is so strong that even if they are tempted to sin again, they don't because their mind is made up that they will never do it again. Before repenting, they might have loved the sin. After repenting, however, they are so revolted by the sin itself that they don't do it. They know the consequences of that sin and want to avoid those results. David, in the story from the last section, is a perfect example of this. When confronted by the prophet Nathan about his sin, David immediately asks God for forgiveness and repents. He hated what he had done and hated that he had upset God. He also did nothing like that ever again.

THE HEART

Both accounts of Saul and David show us it is ultimately the heart that determines if we are a slave of sin. Saul had a hardened heart. He did not love God enough to change his views and ways of doing things. His fleshly nature made him a slave. He was full of pride, fear, and impatience.

David, unlike Saul, was a man after God's own heart. He loved God and hated displeasing Him. Yes, he did mess up and allowed his sexual lust to control him for a moment, but he asked for forgiveness and repented. He changed his mind and actions in order to be closer to God and follow His ways.

In the end, Saul messed up in the same way twice without repenting and lost the kingdom. David messed up and gave into his fleshly desire for women. He repented, though, and changed. Even though he might have been tempted again; he didn't. His legacy, because of his heart after God, included being the ancestor of the Messiah, Jesus.

The same can be said of us. Once we are aware of our fleshly tendencies, our response to the temptations that draw out those fleshly desires will bring light to where our heart is. If our hearts are after Christ, we will not be a slave to sin. This shows we have a heart of repentance. If our hearts are hardened, however, we will continue to allow the flesh to control us in the moments of temptation. The good thing is, as I've said before, we have a helper called the Holy Spirit. If we allow Him to, He helps and strengthens us in those moments of weakness.

His grace is sufficient

As we follow Christ, we don't have to bear the responsibility of making sure we don't mess up. When we try to DO things in our own power to not mess up, we will end up messing up. But, when we simply learn to BE followers of Jesus, we let Him do what He does best. He takes the responsibility for cleaning us up and making us more like Him. Yes, we are a work in progress and we will fail in our journey. The key, however, is to not try to do things on our own. Paul puts it this way in 2 Corinthians 12:9-10

> *"And He said to me, 'My grace is sufficient for you,*
> *for My strength is made perfect in weakness.'*
> *Therefore, most gladly, I will rather boast in my*
> *infirmities, that the power of Christ may rest*
> *upon me. Therefore, I take pleasure in infirmities,*
> *in reproaches, in needs, in persecutions, in*

distresses, for Christ's sake. For when I am weak, then I am strong."

In those moments of temptation, if our hearts are in the right place, all we have to do is call out to the Holy Spirit. His presence will wash over us and purify us. Where before we were slaves to sin and would give in to the desire, we would now have His strength renewing our resolve and longing to please God and follow His ways. We must have a repentant mindset, dependent on Him.

PERSONALITY TYPES

I mentioned earlier in this chapter that I wanted to talk about personality types and how they relate to the battle between the flesh and the spirit. Before I do, I want to emphasize that this is not an exact science. The personality theories aren't always accurate for every person. We are all different and changing. Still, I feel that discussing personality types can be useful in helping us recognize our fleshly tendencies to know how to counter them.

There are three major personality type theories out there that I think are really interesting and can be helpful in our journey to BE like Christ: the Enneagram, the Meyers-Briggs personality types, and the four temperaments introduced by Greek philosopher Hippocrates. I will not get much into each of these in this section. However, I suggest researching them on your own in order to grow in self-awareness.

The main thing I want to emphasize in this small section is that it is good to be aware of the strengths and weaknesses of your personality type. Knowing them gives us an understanding of how to recognize how the flesh influences each of us.

In someone who is more of an authoritative personality type, the flesh comes out in impatience, unkindness, or unloving speech and behavior. For another person who is a fun loving personality type, the flesh can come out in drunkenness, revelry, or sexual immorality. They want to live life "free" to do whatever brings them pleasure. In another person who is quiet and reserved, the flesh could come out in outbursts of wrath. Reserved people rarely like conflict, so they spend so much time bottling in anger at everything that eventually it explodes. These are just a few examples. Again, they are not 100% accurate. Each of the mentioned personality theories is an excellent tool to gain understanding and self-awareness of how the flesh might influence us and how to counter it.

GOD'S WAY

I want to summarize this chapter by giving a practical way to look at the difference between our wills versus God's will.

Our will, influenced by our fleshly nature, is basically this: we want the easy way with the least amount of pain and the most pleasure. It will ultimately cause us pain in the long run because it is not lasting. It will lead to our death and destruction.

Following God's will takes discipline and patience. The journey might be hard, but will eventually get more enjoyable the more we practice His way. It will also lead to the best result possible and our perfection.

No matter who we are, what our personality type is, or what fleshly tendency we are prone to, we have to fall more in love with Him. We also have to bring our minds and lives into submission to the Holy Spirit. We also must learn to surrender our desire to DO things ourselves in our own power. Instead, let us BE His followers and let Him DO the work in us. He covers our sins with His love and strengthens our weaknesses by transforming our minds. What we were once weak in, He pours Himself into and we become strong. If we are unloving and unkind before we encounter Him, we become kind. We become patient if we are impatient. If we loved and sought pleasure, He gives us self-control and a new joy to experience life the way He wants. It's up to us to crucify our fleshly desires and tendencies every day, and choose to take up our cross and follow Jesus obediently.

CHAPTER 3
COMMUNICATING WITH GOD

Discerning God's voice and His will are the most important parts of a Christian's life. How do you hear God's voice and know His will, though? I've been asked that many times. The answer is simple: through developing a lifestyle of prayer and scripture reading. I mentioned both in the last two chapters. They are the two most important spiritual practices available for our spiritual growth. Every follower of Jesus should make them a priority in their lives.

The problem is both prayer and scripture reading are very hard practices to master. Both can seem tedious, especially if you don't understand the importance of them and how they can benefit your life with Christ. Prayer can just seem like talking to the air. There could be several reasons for this. Maybe you have never experienced the presence of God before. Another reason is you might have a bad perspective or understanding of how or what to pray. Scripture reading can be boring, especially if you don't understand what you are reading.

Fortunately, we have a guide that will help us along the way. The Holy Spirit who was sent to be our Helper. Scripture says that He reveals the hidden things of God and helps us understand the mysteries of Scripture. He wants to help us break free from the tediousness of practicing prayer and reading scripture. He does this by opening our eyes to the truth and instilling new faith inside of us.

I want to spend the rest of the next few chapters breaking down both practices. My goal is to help us all understand how we can develop an ear to hear God's voice. We gain this understanding by making these practices a part of our daily walks with Jesus. I want to do this while emphasizing the point of this book. We need to not just DO things to be better Christians. We need to BE His followers growing more and more like Him.

The practices of scripture reading and praying, if done from a DO mindset, will actually hinder your spiritual growth. Those who have this mindset read the Bible and pray from a wrong motive. They do these things for selfish reasons. Some might approach studying scripture to force God to conform to their understanding of who He is and what they want Him to do. They twist scripture to fit their opinions. Praying and Bible reading could also be ways to fulfill the obligation people feel they have as a Christian to pray before meals, bed, work, etc, and read the Bible. Most with this mentality approach these practices as activities to DO in order to be "good Christians," rather than just a natural part of our communication with God. Because of this, they become stuck in the routines of life rather than growing in their relationship with God and experiencing Him in new ways. Some people pray with a selfish motive to get things from God.

Please don't misunderstand what I'm saying. Yes, these are practices we do to help us deepen our relationship with God. We should do them. However, there's a difference between doing them naturally and making them a religious habit to fulfill an obligation. These practices are natural ways to communicate with God, not chores we have to do. It's the same as talking to our friends or family and hanging out with them. It's not a chore for most of us to talk to and hang out with our friends and family. We love doing that, even if we are introverted. The same should be said of our relationship with God. We should love to hang out and talk with Him. When we learn to BE followers of Jesus, these practices become part of who we are. We will develop a desire to talk to Him through prayer and learn from Him through reading scripture. It will become more natural for us as we make these practices a daily habit and learn to listen to His voice and allow Him to teach us.

PRAYER-COMMUNICATION WITH GOD

"Communication is key." We've all heard this phrase from relation-ship experts in TED Talks, relationship blogs, our moms and dads when they're talking to us about our relationship problems, our friends, or some random person on the street. It's a very popular saying. It is a completely accurate statement, though. Healthy communication is the best way to grow our relationships.

What about our relationship with God? Is communication key to our relationship with Jesus? If you follow Jesus or have been to church at all in your life, then you know the answer is yes. It's just a different word that we have used to define communication with God. We use the word prayer. Prayer is communication with God. It is a spiritual discipline we must develop and be consistent with in order to become who we are truly meant to be.

So what makes up healthy communication? Well, as someone who has a bachelor's degree in interpersonal communication and has taken many classes about communication, I can tell you that communication comprises a few parts. To keep it simple, I'll mention four parts:

1. a sender
2. a receiver
3. a message
4. a response

The sender sends a message to the receiver. The receiver receives the message and then responds. For a follower of Jesus, we are the sender who sends messages to God as prayers. God is the receiver who hears our prayers. He then responds by answering them.

WHAT ARE YOU SAYING?

There are two important questions we have to ask ourselves in determining how healthy our prayer life is: "What am I communicating to God?" and "What is God communicating with me?" I want to focus on the question "What am I communicating to God?" in this chapter. Answering this question will determine how healthy/effective your prayer/message sent to God is. It will also determine what His response to it will be and why He responds the way He does.

- *The Heart's Motive*

Communications studies show that around 95% of our communication is nonverbal (facial expressions, body language, tone of voice, and eye contact, to name a few). The other 5% is verbal. This means that the verbal message that we send can sometimes be twisted by the nonverbal messages we send. Because of this, we will sometimes get a response from the sender that we don't understand or like. A good example of this is a server. If a server isn't smiling, has a frown on their face, is throwing food around, etc while they are talking friendly, then the message that they are conveying isn't consistent with their words. The response from the customer will probably be less of a tip or even complaining to the manager. It works the same way in our prayers.

If our hearts aren't in the right place and our actions don't line up with our prayers to God, our message to Him isn't being received the way we'd like it to. That's why selfish/me centered prayers rarely get answered. (Like praying for a corvette or a million dollars). However, when our heart posture is humble and our actions and words reflect our desire to see His kingdom come and others grow, our prayers will be heard and answered the way we want them to.

- *Your Perspective Matters*

Our perspectives and experiences can shape the message being conveyed as well. How you see the person you're talking to can shape the content of the message you're sending. I'm going to talk to my brother much differently than I am a stranger, even if it might be about the same thing. I'm also going to talk much differently to my wife than I will to my brother. They are two unique personalities and have different roles in my life. Also, if my brother has offended me, the message that I send to him will be affected by that offense. The same is true in our prayers to God. Here's a few examples of perspectives that I have heard from people that shape their prayer lives and communication to God:

- God doesn't care about my needs or wants.
- God already knows my needs and wants, so I don't need to ask or talk to Him about them.
- I'm not worthy of getting my prayers answered, so I will not pray.

- I don't know how or what to pray, so I will not pray.
- I know God cares about my prayers, but they seem too small for Him to worry about, so I hate to ask them. (scared/timid prayers)

What we are praying and how we pray matters. If our perspective of God, ourselves, or the purpose of the prayers themselves is unhealthy or unscriptural, then our prayers and what we are communicating are ineffective. They will not be answered. However, if our prayers line up with scripture and come from a healthy perspective, God will hear and respond the way we need it most. Scripture has an answer to combat each of these negative, unhealthy perspectives.

- 1 Peter 5:7 - God cares about your worries and anxious thoughts and wants to hear them.
- Philippians 4:6, Hebrews 4:15-16, John 14:13-14, Matthew 7:7-12, Luke 11: 5-13,18:1-8, James 4:2-3 - God wants us to approach Him boldly with our requests no matter how big or small so that He can be glorified when He answers them. He also wants you to ask persistently.
- Ephesians 2:8-9, 1 John 1:9, James 5:16 - None of us are worthy. However, He makes us worthy through His grace when we confess our sins to Him. We are made righteous (in right standing) through His grace. Because of this, our prayers are effective, no matter what we've done.
- Luke 11:1-5- God is our heavenly Father and wants us to approach Him as a son/daughter to a Father. Also, this is where Jesus shows us how to pray.

When we pray from a mindset that is based on these above scriptures, it takes a lot of the pressure off of us to pray formally or even fearfully, like we might have in the past. Yes, God is bigger than we are and deserves respect, but He is also our Father. If our relationship with Him is as a son/daughter to a father, we don't have to be scared that He won't hear us. You might feel unworthy, think He doesn't care, or won't listen to your prayers. But in fact, it's the opposite. You are His and He loves to hear from you. He listens and wants to respond. When we understand this, we can form the messages/prayers we communicate out of love for Him, thankfulness for what He has done for us, and praise and worship for who He is. We are praying from hearts that have been transformed and have a healthy perspective of who He is. When we believe this, our verbal and nonverbal communication will fully communicate what we need and desire. It will line up with what He wants to do for us. His response will always be the best answer.

- *How Do I Pray?*

> *"Now it came to pass, as He was praying in a*
> *certain place, when He ceased, that one of His*
> *disciples said to Him, 'Lord, teach us to pray, as*
> *John also taught his disciples.' So He said to*
> *them, 'When you pray, say: Our Father in*
> *heaven, Hallowed be Your name. Your kingdom*
> *come. Your will be done On earth as it is in*
> *heaven. Give us day by day our daily bread. And*
> *forgive us our sins, For we also forgive everyone*
> *who is indebted to us. And do not lead us into*
> *temptation, But deliver us from the evil one.'"*

LUKE 11:1-4.

"How do I pray?"

"What do we pray?"

These are great questions that I'm sure every follower of Jesus has asked. First followers of Jesus asked these questions, as illustrated in the above verses that we know as the Lord's Prayer. Not knowing how or what to pray is one of the biggest reasons some people don't pray or have ineffective communication with God. If you hope to grow in your prayer life so that you can learn to hear the voice of God and know His will for your life, I want to ask you the same question I asked in the previous section. "What are you saying and communicating with God?"

What you say in the messages that you communicate to the people in your life determines how healthy your relationships are. A good example of this is verbally abusive spouses/friends versus loving friends and family. Verbally abusive people communicate unhealthy messages, resulting in unhealthy relationships. Loving messages result in loving relationships. Another example of an unhealthy relationship is friends that got offended because of a miscommunication of something from one to another. Their relationship became unhealthy because of an unhealthy message. A lack of communication results in an unhealthy relationship. An example of this is a marriage where both people drifted apart because they didn't communicate.

The same can be said of our relationship with Jesus. What we say or don't say in our message/prayer to God determines how healthy our relationship with God is. In this section, I want to break apart what Jesus is teaching in the Lord's prayer and give some practical practices that can help us understand what to pray and how to pray it so that our relationship with Jesus can grow.

- Our Father in heaven- shows that God is a personal Father and that we can approach Him as a father when we pray.
- Hallowed be Your name- describes who God is and honoring Him.

- Your kingdom come, Your will be done on earth as it is in heaven- recognize God's Lordship and put Him in a position of authority over your life.
- Give us our daily bread- recognize that He is the source of life and He provides us with what we need to thrive.
- forgive our sins- we recognize our sins and our need for a savior who forgives so we confess our sins
- We forgive those who sin against us- we recognize that we have to forgive those who have wronged us or we won't be forgiven. We forgive them or ask God to help us forgive them.
- Do not lead us into temptation but deliver us from evil- We recognize that God never tempts us because He is good. We also recognize that we go through temptation and need Him to deliver us from it.

In these verses, Jesus gives us a clear picture of what it looks like to communicate with God. Something that I want to point out, though, is that not every prayer is going to look exactly like this. I believe that Jesus' purpose behind this prayer wasn't to give us a prayer to copy to fulfill our religious obligation to pray. Instead, He was giving us a model of ideas and things we can say when we are communicating with God. The rest of scripture emphasizes these types of prayers as well. I want to take a few minutes to break down the prayers into more of a practical format we can all apply to our own lives as we follow Christ.

- Petition prayers- These are prayers for any needs or wants in any area of life. We boldly bring our requests to God, knowing He cares for us and wants to hear us ask Him so that He can get glory by answering them. Yes, He might not answer them the way we want Him to or when we want Him to, but we still bring them to Him, knowing He gives us the desires of our hearts and supplies our needs. (Philippians 4:6,19, James 5:13-18, 1 Peter 5:7, Psalm 37:4)

- Repentance/confession prayers- These are prayers that we make recognizing that we have done something wrong. We are turning to God to express our repentance, need for forgiveness, and to ask Him to change our hearts and make us more like Him. (Psalm 51)
- Prayers of lament- These are prayers expressing feelings of grief and sorrow, usually for injustices that have been done or corruption in the world or our hearts. (Psalm 13)
- Intercessory prayer- This type of prayer can go along with prayers of lament and petition prayers but are usually prayers for the needs, salvation, or deliverance of others or nations. We are praying on their behalf. (In Genesis 18, Moses prayed and God saved Lot even though He still destroyed Sodom and Gomorrah)
- Prayers of praise and thanksgiving- These are prayers of celebration and reverence for who God is, describing His character and thankfulness for what He has done. In the Bible, there are seven words that are expressions of celebration. They have action words attached to them as well, including singing, playing instruments, shouting, dancing, lifting hands, bragging about them, blessing them, and to show affection for. So our actions and the songs we sing and play can communicate prayers of praise as well (most of the Psalms).
- Praying in tongues- This type of prayer is probably the most misunderstood and mis-taught. Tongues, along with its counterpart interpretation of tongues, is one of the 9 spiritual gifts mentioned in 1 Corinthians 12. This gift can only be used when a person has been filled or baptized in the Holy Spirit (Acts 2, 10, and 19). It is prayer language

that comes from the Holy Spirit, where He prays through us in a language that we do not know or understand. Unless spoken out loud for all to hear along with an interpretation, it is meant for our personal edification according to 1 Corinthians 14 and for when we don't know what to pray according to Romans 8:26. (I will have more explanation of this gift and how it is to be used in the sequel to this book, *You BE You*.)

These types of prayers don't have to be long or drawn out, formal, or religious prayers. They can intertwine with each other depending on what you are praying for and truly communicate what you are feeling or needing. God wants to hear our prayers. The more we grow in our discipline of praying without ceasing like the Bible says to do in 1 Thessalonians 5:16-18, the better the content of our messages. I would encourage you who are reading this not to look at this as a formula for perfect prayers. Instead, look at it as a challenge to pray deeper, more meaningful prayers that truly express what's going on inside of your heart and life. The closer you get to God, the deeper your prayer life will go. You'll start getting the answers and seeing the results you're looking for and that God wants you to have.

ARE YOU LISTENING

As I mentioned above, prayer is communication with God. Communication requires a sender who sends a message and a receiver who receives the message and then responds. For this next section, I want to ask this question. "Are you listening?"

Listening is an important part of healthy communication and is especially important to developing an effective, growing prayer life. Effective listening requires a few things:

- Did you hear the message being sent or the response to your message? If you didn't hear it in the first place, something is wrong with your ears. You might be deaf or you weren't paying attention to the message. Jesus challenges us to develop an ability and desire to listen to His voice by saying all throughout scripture "He who has ears let him hear."
- If you heard the message, what was your response? The response to the message determines whether you understood or will respond to it the correct way or not.

I want to spend the rest of this section looking at what communication theory says about healthy listening. We must learn to listen. Learning to listen will deepen our understanding of prayer and help us develop ears to hear God's voice.

There is a major difference between hearing and listening. Hearing is perceiving sound. Listening, however, is paying attention to what you hear, considering it, and then responding to what you hear. So, applying this to our spiritual lives, we have to not only develop an ear to hear the voice of God, but also intently listen to it as well. Just because you hear the voice of God doesn't mean you are listening to it. The distinction is whether you focus on Him and His word in order to understand what He is saying and then respond in obedience. Communication theory describes two types of listeners that emphasize this distinction: active listeners and passive listeners.

Active listeners are those who hear a message and pay careful attention to the words spoken. They then respond accordingly. They prepare themselves to listen, consciously observing and thinking about the message being sent. Then they carefully plan an appropriate response. Unlike active listeners, passive listeners hear the message without reacting. They might be distracted and not actually fully hearing what's being said, or they just didn't care to focus fully on the message. Either way, the response is still the same. They do not respond. Jesus puts it this way in Matthew 7: 24-27.

> *"Therefore whoever hears these sayings of Mine, and does them, I will liken him to a wise man who built his house on the rock: and the rain descended, the floods came, and the winds blew and beat on that house; and it did not fall, for it was founded on the rock. But everyone who hears these sayings of Mine, and does not do them, will be like a foolish man who built his house on the sand: and the rain descended, the floods came, and the winds blew and beat on that house; and it fell. And great was its fall."*

Jesus is saying something very important to us in this passage. We must have hearts that will actively listen to His voice and respond by applying His teachings in every area of our lives. Those who do this are wise and have a good foundation. They will stand firm even in the storms. Those who hear, but don't respond in obedience are foolish people who have an unstable foundation. They will be blown away by the slightest wind.

A perfect example of active listening versus passive listening in the Bible is in 1 Samuel 3. Samuel heard God's voice calling his name three times. The first two times, he didn't understand that it was God trying to get his attention. After the counsel of Eli, though, he recognized it was God and responded to His voice. He spent time with Him, actively listening to understand what God was telling him. It was at this moment that Samuel went from being a young boy who didn't know the voice of God, to hearing His voice for the first time. This moment was the beginning of a journey with God that would cause Samuel to become one of the greatest prophets in the Bible. He went from unintentional passive listener to intentional active listener.

I want to ask this question again to challenge us to examine our prayer lives. "Are you listening?" Are you able to hear the voice of God? Are your spiritual ears open? If they are and you can hear Him, are you a passive listener or an active listener? Do you respond to the voice of God, or do you choose to ignore it? My hope and prayer is that we can all become active listeners to the voice of God, longing to hear His voice and feel His presence, walking with Him in love and obedience in order to truly BE like Him in every way.

COMMUNICATION IS KEY

My challenge I leave with you echoes the words of Jesus "He who has ears let Him hear." Fall in love with Jesus and His teachings. Walk in obedience. Don't just pray for the sake of saying religious words to show that you are a good Christian. BE a follower of Jesus and let these healthy spiritual communication practices grow in your life naturally as He reveals Himself to you when you seek Him. Speak to God confidently. Speak exactly what it is you want to communicate. Then actively listen for His voice. As you grow in this practice, you will learn to hear and understand what He is saying. What is God saying to you when you listen? I will talk more about this in the next chapter.

CHAPTER 4
THE VOICE OF GOD

Throughout all of Scripture, we see God speaking to His people. Abraham was known as a friend of God and talked with God regularly. Moses heard God's voice in a burning bush. Later, God spoke to him on Mount Sinai. It was at this moment that God established the law by giving Moses the Ten Commandments. Elijah heard the voice of God in a still, small voice. God spoke to the prophets through prophecies proclaiming judgment, restoration, and the coming Messiah. Jesus, God made flesh, spoke to the disciples, teaching them about the Kingdom of Heaven.

Scripture isn't the only way He speaks, though. Something that many believers in our modern society have forgotten is that God still speaks to His people today. In the last chapter, I talked about active and passive listening. I asked, "Are you listening?" I want to ask the same question along with this challenge that Jesus gives us in Matthew 11:15. "He who has ears let him hear." He is speaking. Are we listening? If so, what is He saying?

GOD STILL SPEAKS

One misconception that some in the church have is that God does not speak the same way He used to. This isn't true, though. The Bible says in Hebrews 13:8 that "Jesus Christ is the same yesterday, today, and forever." He hasn't changed since the dawn of time. If He hasn't changed according to scripture, why would He change the way He speaks? The answer is obvious. He still speaks the same way today that He did to His followers in the Old Testament. The question is, are we listening? So, how does God speak to us?

THE WRITTEN WORD-SCRIPTURE

The first way that God speaks to us today is through what the ancient Greeks called the *logos*, or the written word. These words, recorded in what we know as the Bible, were what God had spoken to His people in the past. These words were passed down from generation to generation.

So how is God speaking to us through Scripture? Is it still relevant for us today 2000 years after it was actually written?

Paul says in 2 Timothy 3:16-17 that all Scripture is "God breathed and is useful for teaching, rebuking, correcting, and training for righteousness, so that the servant of God may be thoroughly equipped for every good work." This means that the Bible is the very word or voice of God. Yes, it was recorded by humans, but every word came from God Himself. He speaks to us through these written words to show us who He is and teach us to live the way He wants us to live. These words show us how to BE like Him. The question we have to ask ourselves, though, is are we listening? Do we read the Bible and hear God's voice clearly through the writings? Or are they just words on pages?

Why Should I Read the Bible?

There are three reasons Christians today don't read the Bible. They don't agree with teachings in it, understand the relevance of it today, or they don't understand what it is saying. Unfortunately, part of the reason that so many people don't read the Bible is that church leaders haven't explained why the Bible is so important to read. They also haven't taught how to study it. They say that people should read it, but don't explain why or how. Thus, the Bible is now a mantle decoration gathering dust in people's homes.

So why should we read the Bible? There are several important reasons to study Scripture.

The first and most important reason is this: it is God speaking to us about Himself. It is a letter from a creator to His creation, a Father to His children, telling us who He is. In this letter, He shows us how much He loves us, what He has done for us, and what He wants to do for us. Sometimes a son or a daughter who never knew their father or had a poor father will grow up with certain character flaws. These traits will prevent them from being healthy in various areas of life. How much more so for someone who doesn't know their heavenly Father? The One who created them and has a perfect plan of wholeness that He wants to share with them. The Bible is this plan laid out and given to us. If we never read it, we will never know our Father. We will never be whole if we don't know Him.

The second reason I want to give to help us understand why we should read the Bible is for those who are a little more skeptical about the Bible's validity. The Bible was written by over 40 authors from different walks of life over a period of over 1400 years. Yet it maintains complete consistency. There are also various architectural findings and historical accounts proving the stories and authorship validity. This shows that, even though there were many people who wrote in the Bible, there is one Author who spoke the words to the people who recorded them. This points us back to my first reason.

God is speaking to us about His love and plan through these words. If you are still skeptical about this book and it's Author I would say, "why not give it a shot?" It's the greatest letter ever written and is filled with truths that are still relevant today. Also, just as a side note, if you believe in social justice and humanitarian efforts, you might find that Jesus is a huge advocate for social justice and love. In fact, a lot of the social justice programs we have today have their roots in Christianity/Judaism and from the Scriptures. Read it with an open mind and research the findings and accounts for yourself, proving its validity and literary accuracy.

The third reason I want to give is for those who already believe in God and want to follow Jesus. Paul tells Timothy that Scripture is "useful for teaching, rebuking, correcting, and training for righteousness, so that the servant of God may be thoroughly equipped for every good work." The Bible says in Hosea 4:6 that God's people are destroyed because of their lack of knowledge. The Israelites had forgotten God's laws that He had given them. As a result, they turned away from Him, bringing about their own destruction. The same is true for us today if we don't know what God says about things. In the first chapter of this book, I mentioned some of the false teachings that the church today believes. I also said that it was important that we study scripture to know who God is. It is important to add that when we study scripture, we find truth. Jesus said in John 8:32 that the truth sets us free. So when we don't study scripture, we will never be free from our struggles and sin. We won't know how to follow Jesus and learn how to respond to temptation. We also won't be equipped to fulfill the purpose that God has for us if we don't read scripture. God has given us the answer to every question, trial, and sin struggle in His word. If we take the time to read it, we will learn the truth and find the freedom we need to BE like Jesus.

How Do I Study the Bible?

Now that I have given reasons for you to consider why you should read the Bible, I want to say that reading the Bible is difficult if you are not prepared. I mentioned some reasons that people don't read the Bible. The Bible is hard to understand. Also, some believe the Bible isn't applicable today. To both, I would say, "yes it is." Yes, it is hard to understand and yes, it does apply to our lives today. The reason people think it is hard to understand or misunderstand the way it applies is because they don't know how to study it correctly.

The Bible is filled with truths and wisdom that will help us. In order to learn them, though, we have to study Scripture. We will never learn their meaning and application if we don't understand one very important element of Bible study: context, context, context. To understand scripture, we have to understand the context of the scripture. There are a few different context clues we look for when studying scripture: historical/cultural/geographical context and literary context. A method that I have used to find out the context is the WHO, WHAT, WHEN, WHERE, WHY, HOW method.

- WHO- who wrote it, who did he/she write it to, who is it about?
- WHAT- what was he/she saying?
- WHEN- What time period was the author in when they wrote it? What was the culture like? What were the historical events that were happening in this time period and why do they matter?
- WHERE-What nation did they live in? What language did he/she speak and write in originally and is the translation completely accurate? (side note: Old Testament was in Hebrew and the New Testament was in Greek. English translations don't give full meaning to words, so it's important to research what words mean in those original languages when studying the Bible.)

- WHY-Why did the author write what he/she wrote?
- HOW- How can we apply it today?

This method is just one way to approach studying Scripture. There are lots of different materials and books on bible study methods that would be worth looking at. I would encourage you to check them out and find what works for you to get the most out of your time studying scripture.

Meditation

Another practice that I want to mention that goes well with Scripture reading is meditation.

What pops into your mind when I say meditation? Some of you might picture a guru sitting cross-legged on the floor with his fingers crossed, eyes closed, and humming. You might even be freaking out, thinking that I might be a crazy person teaching some kind of heresy. I want to calm all of those fears right now, though. The practice of meditation is helpful in growing your relationship with God. Yes, some forms of meditation have been aligned with occultism and demonic practices in the past. However, there is a biblical model for this practice. King David, an ancestor of Jesus and the one person in the Bible that God says was "a man after His own heart" practiced meditation.

In other religions, meditation is used to clear the mind to reach a level of spiritual euphoria and awareness. Buddhists use meditation to reach a state of complete calmness that can lead to "enlightenment." Others use meditation to reach the spiritual realm in order to speak to spirits, as with some practices of witchcraft and Hinduism.

Biblical meditation, though, is more than just finding a state of calmness to center yourself. It's about focusing your attention completely on God. David mentioned meditating throughout the Psalms. In Psalm 119:15, he says,

> *"I will meditate on Your precepts, and contemplate*
> *Your ways."*

The word meditate that he uses here is the Hebrew word *siyach*, which means to ponder, think on, or to mutter to yourself about what you are thinking or reading about. What David is saying here is that he was pondering or contemplating on the ways of God. He was reminding himself of them by speaking the truth aloud to himself. We can definitely learn from this example and apply it to our own lives. Meditation forces us to take our minds off of worldly things or the struggles of life and put them on God, remembering who He is. Paul emphasizes this principle in two different scriptures. In Colossians 3:2 he says

> *"Set your mind on things above, not on things on the*
> *earth"*

and in Romans 10:17

> *"So then faith comes by hearing, and hearing by the*
> *word of God."*

So while you are reading scripture, practice this form of meditation and think about what you are reading. Speak it to yourself in order to remind yourself of who God is and ponder on its application in your life. Your faith will increase as you ponder and speak aloud the Word of God.

Living and Powerful

One last thing I want to mention is that the Word of God is living and powerful. It is still just as applicable today as it was over the past 4,000 years. If you allow it to, it will reveal truths about yourself and about God that you didn't know. My prayer for those who read this is that you will find a hunger for God's word so deep that it is like Jeremiah describes. "A fire shut up in my bones that I cannot contain" (Jeremiah 20:9) and that David describes as a yearning "like a deer panting for the water brooks." (Psalm 42:1.)

THE SPOKEN WORD

The other way that God speaks is through what the Greeks called the *rhema*, or spoken word. This way of God speaking is supernatural and can only come out of having healthy communication or prayer life with Him. As I mentioned in the previous chapter, prayer is communication with God. Communication requires a sender who sends a message to a receiver who then responds, depending on how healthy the message was.

Effective communication requires us to be face to face with the person we are talking to. I know that in today's society we have cell phones, postal services, email, social media, Skype, FaceTime, Zoom, etc as modes of communication. However, the best, most effective mode of communication that we have is communicating face to face. In any of the other modes, the message will be distorted and not received properly. Spiritually, we only have one mode of communication with God. Prayer. Think of it this way: prayer is like if every other mode of communication in today's society was taken away. Cell phones gone, no online access to Skype, Zoom, or to send email, no postal service to send letters back and forth, no social media to follow and talk with friends on. The only way you could communicate with someone is if you physically go to that person and talk with him/her face to face. Fortunately for us, God is everywhere and is always listening and responding. Even if we don't see or hear Him. All we have to do is talk to Him and listen when He talks back.

So what does that look like since we can't literally be face to face with God? He's a spirit and we can't see Him. Also, God is omnipresent or everywhere at the same time, so aren't we already in His presence? The answer to both is this: yes, God is everywhere. We cannot hide from Him. However, even though He is there, we cannot sense Him. Our senses are closed off to His presence because of our sin nature. So, in order for us to experience and sense His presence, He has to reveal Himself to us and open our senses so that we can encounter Him. A perfect example of this is the burning bush found in Exodus 3. Moses encounters God for the first time and speaks to Him there.

God wants to reveal Himself and speak to us just like He did in Scripture. We just have to pay attention, listening for when HE speaks. Sometimes He shows up blatantly and unexpectedly, like with Moses, and other times He shows up in a still, peaceful way that could be easily missed. A perfect example of this is in 1 Kings 19:11-13. Elijah was commanded by God to go to the mountain of God in Horeb and wait for Him to come. So Elijah obeyed. While he was waiting, there was a strong wind that broke the rocks, an earthquake, and fire. God's presence was not in any of those dynamic occurrences. His presence came as a still, small voice. In that moment, after hearing that voice, Elijah knew God had come. He could have doubted, but because He had already experienced the presence of God and had developed an awareness of what that presence felt and sounded like, he was ready to meet with God and listen to His voice. Just like Elijah, we need to train ourselves to be aware of His presence so that we won't miss when He shows up and speaks.

So what is His presence like? I want to give two scenarios that will help give us a perspective of what the presence of God could be like. Picture in your mind two images.

- *Majestic King*

Picture in your mind's eye this first scenario: a king who is walking around his palace. He is obviously a king and in control. He is dressed in full majesty and glory. When he walks into a room, his very presence causes people to stand at attention. Even those not from his kingdom feel the weight of that presence and either come to love and respect him, just like his subjects, or hate him and fear him. Those who hear him do what he says because of the love they have for him. They want to be near him because they know that when he is there; he brings blessing and peace. His enemies tremble in His presence. When he comes in battle, they turn and run to avoid the awesomeness of his glory and strength.

- *Loving Father*

The second scenario: The same king. He is eating with his beloved children, spending time with them, listening to how their day went, letting them vent all their frustrations at how angry a friend of theirs made them, or how much they hate math. He draws the youngest daughter onto his lap and whispers into her ear. The daughter smiles and whispers something back. He then tickles her as she giggles and squirms. The oldest son asks for permission to ride horses the next day and the king says yes, take the best horse. It's yours. The son grins, runs up and says "thank you, thank you, thank you!" The middle son asks the king to teach him how to sword fight and the king says "when you're older son."

This is what being in God's presence is like. We are His children that He wants the best for, loves to spend time with, give wonderful gifts to, and whisper secrets to. We are His servants that notice His presence and stand at attention immediately when He walks into the room and obey when He commands something.

BE WITH GOD

Some of you might ask why I gave these scenarios and what they have to do with this topic. A healthy prayer life begins with being with God. Just like you can't communicate with someone that you're not with, you can't communicate effectively with God if you're not first experiencing His presence. The key to experiencing God's presence is to develop an awareness of it. The more aware you are, the easier it is to notice when He comes and reveals Himself. These two images are perfect pictures of who God is and how He interacts with His people. He is a loving parent and a majestic, mighty, and just ruler. He breathes stars into existence, speaks life where there was none. He knows each of us by name and loves us with an unfailing love. He wants to give us our hearts desire when we trust and follow Him. His presence brings freedom to those who follow Him and terror to those who don't. This is the truth about who God is. We only learn this through being with Him.

As we continue to grow in His presence as we meet with Him, we also hear His rhema word. He speaks to our hearts through the Holy Spirit, bringing conviction, renewal, and revealing scripture to us as we study. He also speaks to us through the spiritual gifts listed in 1 Corinthians 12. I want to highlight the ones that are specifically messages from the Holy Spirit. They are supernatural messages given through a believer and can be spoken or written. They are word of wisdom, word of knowledge, prophecy, tongues, and inter-pretation of tongues.

- Word of wisdom- the Holy Spirit uses a believer to give supernatural advice and wisdom about a situation that they previously had no answer for. This wisdom can only come through divine inspiration. An example of this is James in Acts 5:13-21, when the apostles were deciding if the Gentiles needed to be circumcised or not. He gives a Holy Spirit inspired answer to their question.
- Word of knowledge- when the Holy Spirit gives a believer insight about a person or situation that they did not know previously. An example of this in the Bible is in Act 5 when the Holy Spirit revealed to Peter that Ananias and Sapphira were lying about how much they had sold their property for.
- Prophecy- a supernatural message from God through someone that brings revelation of sin and the need for repentance. It is also a message of encouragement to believers. It can also be a message foretelling future events like the prophecies in the Old Testament about the Messiah or a message to someone about hidden sin. Nathan talking to David about his adultery with Bathsheba in order to get him to repent is an example of this.
- Tongues- this gift is the most confusing and controversial gift in the Bible. Simply put, the gift of tongues is the Holy Spirit praying and speaking through a believer to bring encouragement to that person. It is available for every believer to strengthen their own personal relationship with God. Paul says in 1 Corinthians 14 that when we pray in tongues, we edify ourselves. You can pray in tongues anytime and anywhere under the inspiration of the Holy Spirit, but there is an appropriate way to do it when in public. When someone gives a message in tongues corporately, under the influence of the Holy Spirit, it must always come with an

interpretation in order to edify the entire body. Otherwise it's useless.

- Interpretation of tongues- when a message in tongues is given, the Holy Spirit provides an interpretation in order to bring understanding to the people who need to hear it. The interpretation can come in two ways: by every person hearing it in the language that they speak, like on the Day of Pentecost in Acts 2, or by one person giving the interpretation prophetically under the inspiration of the Holy Spirit.

BACK TO THE BASICS

If learning to listen to the voice of God is so important, how do we develop an ear to hear His voice and respond to it? My answer to this question is this: start with the basics and work your way to maturity. Scripture gives us a foundation that applies to all of our lives:

- *Love God*

Luke 10:27 says that we are to love God with every part of who we are.

> *"You shall love the Lord your God with all your heart, with all your soul, with all your strength, and with all your mind."*

The first step in developing an ear for God's voice is to fall in love with Him. We fall in love with Him by listening to the Holy Spirit's voice of conviction. Listening and responding to Him leads to our salvation. This is the moment we begin following Jesus and becoming like Him. The closer we follow Him and learn about

Him, the more we fall in love with Him. When we love Him, we love to hear His voice speaking to us.

- *Love people*

Luke 10:27 ends with the second greatest commandment:

"love your neighbor as yourself."

When we love God and learn to listen to His voice, He speaks to us about His heart for the people in our lives. We start to love them just as much as we love ourselves. If we never get to this point in our love for God that we start to love people, our ears will be closed off to His voice.

- *Search for Him*

The best way to learn His voice is to find out more about who He is. Lucky for us, we have the Bible to read. The Bible is a letter from God to us about who He is, what He has done, and what He wants to do for us. If we want to hear His voice, His scripture is the perfect place to develop an ear to hear.

- *Respond to His word*

As we read what He says in scripture, we should then obey His commands. We find all throughout scripture that those who hear the word of the Lord and then obey it are the ones who thrive in their relationship with God. They go deeper in Him, recognizing when He speaks. When He moves, they move with Him. Those who don't obey eventually stop hearing the voice of God and move against His plan.

- *Be filled with the Spirit*

When we begin the journey with Jesus, the Holy Spirit steps into our lives and begins the process of sanctification. Every believer has access to the Holy Spirit. If we let Him, He will fill us to over-flowing, empowering us to be the best witnesses of the gospel we can be, just like He did on the Day of Pentecost. When we are filled with the Holy Spirit in this way, we learn to listen to His speaking and leading in ways that we could not before. This is a gift that is available for all of us. However, it's our choice to accept it or not. Being filled with the Holy Spirit leads to what we call the gifts of the spirit that Paul mentioned in 1 Corinthians 12 and 14. They can only be used when our ears are completely in tune with the Holy Spirit and are supernatural manifestations of His power.

BEST PRACTICES

These foundational goals given to us in the Bible are for every believer, no matter who you are and what you've done. In order to increase our prayer life beyond this point, we must realize that we are all different. The Holy Spirit speaks to each of us differently. It's up to you to figure out how best you hear God and how He speaks to you. I want to end this section by thinking practically about this in order to help us all grow in our communication with God. Here are a few questions to ask yourself that will help you figure out the best way to learn how to hear God's voice clearly:

What do you do or where do you go to feel God's presence? For me, it's through music and spending time in nature. For others, I know it could be through nature as well, through reading His word, through meditation, or through community with others. What do you do or where do you go to feel God's presence in times of chaos, trials, or struggles, or in times of calm? Can you hear Him speaking to you while you're in His presence?

My challenge to you is if you haven't found a place or a hobby where you best feel God's presence, then find that place. Actively make it a part of your daily life. While in that place, ask God to speak to you so you can develop your spiritual ears to hear His voice. Once you have developed that ear, start practicing listening in other places and doing other things as well until you are a master at hearing God's voice anytime, anyplace, no matter what is going on or what you are doing.

CHAPTER 5
A JOURNEY OF SEASONS

We are all on a journey to BE more like Jesus. Or we should be if we are not. Like I've mentioned in the last few chapters, who we become depends on knowing God and following Him. We learn who He is and develop a healthy relationship with Him through healthy communication practices. We learn His will for our lives as we communicate with Him through prayer and listening to what He says in His word.

Jesus' desire is to take His followers on a journey. While on that journey, He develops us, making us more like Him. We see this in the Gospels as the disciples follow Jesus, learning to apply Kingdom principles taught by God Himself.

In Scripture, we see that many people followed Jesus. Only twelve, however, were the ones who Jesus had called to follow Him. They were Simon (Peter), James (the son of Zebedee), John, Andrew, Bartholomew, James the son of Alpheus, Judas, Thadeus (Jude), Matthew, Phillip, Simon the Zealot, and Thomas. Each of them came from different backgrounds and had unique personalities. As they walked with Jesus, we see that each of them progressed in different ways that changed everything about them.

- *PETER*

Peter was a fisherman who was impulsive and stuck his foot in his mouth several times. He also denied Jesus three times. Despite these weaknesses, Jesus brought him from being a simple, impulsive fisherman to being one of the most prolific fathers of our faith. I will talk more about his journey in a later chapter.

- *JAMES AND JOHN "THE SONS OF THUNDER"*

James and John, the sons of Zebedee, were also fishermen. Scholars believe that they were very confrontational, loud, aggressive people earning them the nickname "sons of thunder." They were the ones who wanted to call down fire on the people of Samaria when they were rejected from the village in Luke 9. Their journey with Jesus transformed them from people who were quick to anger into people of love. In fact, we see that John teaches about love in his epistles.

- *BARTHOLOMEW or NATHANIEL*

Nathaniel, whose name is also mentioned as Bartholomew, was skeptical about Jesus at first. Phillip came to him saying that he had met the Messiah. When Nathaniel heard that, his response was scoffing at the idea that anything good could come out of Nazareth. This showed his bigotry toward Nazarenes. However, once he met Jesus and experienced who He was personally, his mind was changed. He followed Him wholeheartedly.

- *MATTHEW*

Matthew was working as a tax collector when Jesus called him to be His disciple. This decision was more than likely frowned upon by the other disciples at first. Tax collectors were among the most hated people in Israel. They were considered sellouts who worked with the Romans to collect the taxes of the people. They would then take a portion for themselves, making the people see them as thieves as well. This didn't stop Jesus from choosing him, though. Matthew went from being regarded as the lowest of the low to being a founding leader of the early church. He also wrote a record of what happened when Jesus walked the earth. We know this account as the Gospel of Matthew

- *THOMAS*

Thomas was another disciple Jesus had chosen who was also a skeptic. We sometimes refer to him as "Doubting Thomas." He was more of a realist than the others, needing to see it to believe it. That changed, though, when Jesus revealed Himself to Him after His resurrection, letting him touch His scars and side. In this moment, he was changed from a person who needed to see it to believe it to believing in Jesus completely. We see him living out that faith in the book of Acts along with the other disciples, performing signs, wonders, and miracles in the name of Jesus and preaching that He is the Messiah.

- *JUDAS*

There was one disciple, unfortunately, whose life was not completely changed by walking with Jesus. This man was Judas Iscariot, the one who betrayed Jesus. Even though he had seen the miracles Jesus performed and heard His teaching, he did not apply those words to his own life. He never saw Jesus as Lord, only as a teacher. This shows us that even those who start out as followers of

Jesus can still reject the truth if they do not allow themselves to grow and change.

CALLED TO BE FREE

People who have limited lifespans, aren't eternal, and don't possess infinite wisdom and knowledge, unlike God, have to go through life constantly growing and changing. If we don't, we will be stuck in an endless cycle of constant misery, going in circles making the same idiotic mistakes repeatedly. We will most likely make others miserable as well if we aren't careful. We see throughout history that this cycle of stupidity is filled with wars and violence, death, constant betrayal, lies, and drama, drama, drama. And more drama. Lots of drama. Get the picture? Drama. This cycle of stupidity is usually caused by our own fleshly desires. No matter the consequences, we want to do what we want to do when we want to do it. Jesus wants to set us free from the cycles of stupidity, though. He has made a way out of them. He has given us a way to grow and change if we choose to take this journey with Him.

WE ARE CHOSEN

Just like the disciples, Jesus has called us to follow Him. We have the choice to follow Him or not. If we choose to see Him as our Lord and follow Him wholeheartedly, He will develop us into people who are like Him, just like the disciples. He does this by bringing us through different seasons and trials that He uses to shape and purify us. We have the choice to go through those seasons and endure the trials in order to change. This is the only way to experience true freedom and become who He has called us to BE.

These trials will help us grow in the specific areas we struggle in. They will not be easy. In fact, Jesus says that life following Him will be filled with many hardships that will test our faith. James, however, urges us to

> *"count it all joy when you fall into various trials"*

in James 1:2. He continues on by saying,

> *"knowing that the testing of your faith produces patience. But let patience have its perfect work, that you may be perfect and complete, lacking nothing."*

This shows us that God has a purpose for the trials that we go through. He allows us to go through them so that our faith will be strengthened. These trials will lead us closer to Him if we take joy in them. We should recognize that His Spirit is with us, leading us through these seasons and trials. We should also take comfort in knowing that He is perfecting us along the way and making us more like Him.

SEASONS

Life is full of seasons. Each season is designed by God and has a specific purpose. A wise man long ago emphasizes this by saying:

> *"To everything there is a season, a time for every purpose under heaven, a time to be born, and a time to die; a time to plant, and a time to pluck what is planted; a time to kill, and a time to heal; a time to break down, and a time to build up; a time to weep, and a time to laugh; a time to mourn, and a time to dance; a time to cast away stones, and a time to gather stones; a time to*

embrace, and a time to refrain from embracing;
a time to gain, and a time to lose; a time to keep,
and a time to throw away; a time to tear, and a
time to sew; a time to keep silence, and a time to
speak; a time to love, and a time to hate; a time
of war, and a time of peace."

This wise man was King Solomon in Ecclesiastes 3:1-8.

God ordains and designs certain seasons specifically for our growth. He fills them with trials and challenges and uses them to bring about the change needed for us to become who we are supposed to BE. Even as followers of Jesus; we go through these seasons. They are inevitable. Some seasons are harder and longer than others, depending on if we learn the lesson we are supposed to be learning. How we go through them will determine what we learn from them. If our perspective about the season is healthy, then we will go through it with Him guiding and teaching us how to BE like Christ. If it's not, then we will most likely be stuck in a mindset of just DOING the wrong things repeatedly.

Over the next few chapters, I want to discuss a few of the seasons that each of us as followers of Jesus will go through, and how they affect our spiritual growth. Before I go any further, though, I want to mention one spiritual discipline that is given by God to help us in whatever season we're in. This is the practice of community.

COMMUNITY

As I've mentioned in the last few chapters, prayer and scripture reading are the two most important practices that each of us must master in order to know who God is, learn to hear His voice, and learn to BE like Jesus. The practice of community, however, is just as important and necessary for our growth. Paul tells us in 1

LIVE IT. BE IT.

Corinthians 12 that we are the body of Christ and each of us has a role in His body. This means that we are part of the greatest family in the world: the family of God. We are brothers and sisters in Christ, sons and daughters of the Father, and we have a role to play in helping the body become more like Jesus. The practice of community is the practice of staying connected to the body of Christ. We do this by spending time together and building each other up. Paul also tells us in Hebrews 10:23-25 that we are to

> *"hold fast the confession of our hope without waver-*
> *ing, for He who promised is faithful. And let us*
> *consider one another in order to stir up love and*
> *good works, not forsaking the assembling of*
> *ourselves together, as is the manner of some, but*
> *exhorting one another, and so much the more as*
> *you see the Day approaching."*

In other words, we should always be coming together as followers of Jesus and helping each other grow.

This practice is hard to do, however, when society has taught us that we don't need others to succeed. The "American dream" has taught us to pursue our own happiness no matter what. America has become an individualistic society where everyone has a dream to be "successful" and be happy. We do our best to achieve this dream without anyone's help to prove ourselves. We are a very independent, strong-willed people. Our society is designed so that in order to achieve "success" we have to leave our families and friends to go to college, get a degree, then set out to start our career and make a name for ourselves. Usually we do this alone. I personally believe, and I'm sure that others will agree with me, that this individualistic mindset is the reason why our nation is filled with such disunity and why loneliness, depression and anxiety is rising. When we do things alone to achieve our own goals instead of inviting others into our lives and plans to journey with us, we will fall apart. Families are separated and marriages fall apart because one or both adult parents spend so much time working that they don't spend time together. The kids are left to take care of themselves and sometimes get into trouble because they need attention and do bad things to get it.

This mindset has seeped into the church as well. Even though God has called us to do life together and journey with Him just like the disciples did, our church culture has become one where we do life together once a week, if that. We go to church on Sundays and the rest of the week we just focus on ourselves, our families, or our jobs. Some people who claim to be Christian only go on Easter and Christmas. For some, Sundays have become the day for football games, kids' baseball games, day drinking, or "Sunday Fundays." We hear things such as "I don't need to go to church to be a Christian." The problem is we can't become who God called us to BE on our own. God's design is for us to do it together. Paul says it this way in 1 Corinthians 12:26 that when

> *"one member suffers, all the members suffer with it;*
> *or if one member is honored, all the members*
> *rejoice with it."*

This shows us that we are not called to be alone. We are called to do life together.

COMMUNITY OF LOVE

When we go through hard seasons, we need our brothers and sisters there to "bear our burdens" as Paul says in Galatians 6:2. When we experience triumphs and growth, it's always great to have our brothers and sisters there to celebrate with us. This is the point of the practice of community. We go through seasons of growth together so that we can all BE who God has called us to BE. This is how we distinguish ourselves from the rest of the world. While the world acts selfishly and falls apart because there is no community and unity, we, as the body of Christ, are held together by our love for one another. In fact, this is the way that we show that we are followers of Jesus, by demonstrating our love for one another. Jesus said this exact thing in John 13:35.

> *"A new commandment I give to you, that you love one another; as I have loved you, that you also love one another. By this all will know that you are My disciples, if you have love for one another."*

The best act of love that we can show each other is if we journey with Christ together, in unity. We stay in community with each other and make it a habit to put our brothers and sisters first, bearing each other's burdens, rejoicing in the triumphs, and growing together. In fact, practicing community is the best way to find healing and freedom. James 5:16 says that we are to confess our sins to one another and pray for one another to find healing and freedom. We can't do this if we aren't practicing community.

So how do we do this if we are so used to doing things alone or are very independent people? If you want to start making this practice a habit, the best way to do this is through food. Food has a way of bringing people together. Practice mastering the discipline of community by inviting other followers of Jesus into your life with food. Acts 2:46-47 illustrates this perfectly.

> *"So continuing daily with one accord in the temple, and breaking bread from house to house, they ate their food with gladness and simplicity of heart,*

praising God and having favor with all the
people. And the Lord added to the church daily
those who were being saved."

As you take the first step in developing this practice it will become easier to make this a part of your identity. Open up yourself, be vulnerable, and allow others into your life, even if it is a mess. We are all a work in progress, but if we do it together we can truly BE who God has called us to BE.

JOURNEY TOGETHER

As I've said earlier in this chapter, Jesus is calling us to follow Him. As we journey with Him, He brings us through seasons of challenges and trials that are designed to help us BE like Him. They will be difficult, but it is important to remember that we are not alone in these seasons. God has put a community of brothers and sisters into our lives who will journey with us and encourage us through these seasons. As we follow Jesus together, practicing the discipline of community in the easy seasons and the hard, we will become who He has called us to BE.

CHAPTER 6
SEASONS OF CHANGE

Change is inevitable. Life is full of change and transitions. Our own natural seasons demonstrate this. Summer turns to fall, fall turns to winter, winter turns to spring, and then spring turns back into summer and the cycle begins again.

When summer turns to fall, the leaves change colors, the weather changes from warm and sunny to cold and rainy. Starbucks and other fancy coffee shops change their menus to fall themes and bring out the pumpkin spice flavored drinks and snacks that all the "basic white girls" flock to. People change their houses with Halloween or Thanksgiving decorations and colors. Farmers prepare their barns and begin the harvesting process.

Fall to winter changes are similar. All the trees change from colorful and pretty to lifeless. The ground changes from green to brown and muddy or white with snow depending on where you are. People put up Christmas trees and decorations to celebrate the holidays. Stores bring out their sales ads to prepare for the madhouse Black Friday and other Christmas events. After Christmas, the entire world shuts down for the rest of winter. Depending on where they live, people don't go outside anymore because of the cold, rain, and snow,

When winter turns into spring again, we see other major changes happening. The trees and ground turn green, flowers bloom, farmers plant their crops, and animals give birth, restarting the growth of life again that was stopped by winter. Women bring out their colorful spring dresses, men bring out their shorts and polos. New life has begun.

Summer is the fruition of what was started in spring. It is the result of all the changes that occurred during the previous seasons. This is the time where people have fun and enjoy themselves outside in the warm sunshine. They've been inside all winter and can now come and enjoy new life. Life is good.

For a follower of Jesus, change is inevitable. We go through changes constantly, some good and pleasant, some bad and depressing. Whatever the change, it will always have a level of anxiety and stress that comes along with it. It requires us to adapt to the new normal.

Some of us might have experienced or will experience a change in a job or a career. That change might be a good thing, such as getting hired to do a better-paying job or being promoted within the company you already work for. Or it could result from being unwillingly terminated. Both scenarios will most likely have some level of difficulty and stress. They will each have to say goodbye to people they might have had some kind of connection with. The person who willingly left the old job will have the stress of learning the new job. Even if they might be excited about it, it will come with some anxiety. The person who unwillingly has to find a new job has the added stress of filling out applications and going through the interview process before they even start the new job, plus learning all the ins and outs.

Some of you might be feeling the calling to go into a new season of ministry, where God has given you a new dream. I know several missionaries who have experienced this change. They hear the calling to leave everything behind and go to a new place, sometimes thousands of miles from their home, to be and preach Jesus to those who have never heard of Him. I have personally experienced this calling and the change that came with it a few times in my life. This change is hard, especially when you are so far from loved ones. Giving up your own personal comfort and even safety for the sake of being obedient to God is very hard as well.

How you perceive change and how you allow yourself to deal with it determines who you become after change occurs. I will talk about your perspective during hard seasons in a later chapter. For the rest of this chapter, though, I want to talk about the need for change in our lives.

NEW LIFE

The thing to remember about seasons of change is that change always leads to a new life. Growth and new life require change. A seed that is planted has to change from seed form in order to sprout into a tree. For us as followers of Jesus, the first step toward growth is to allow ourselves to be planted in a season of change. The next step after allowing ourselves to be planted where God wants us to be is to endure the change that happens once we are planted. It will be difficult and uncomfortable. Old things and ways of doing things have to die in order for us to change.

The Bible is very clear that there is change involved when we decide to follow Christ. Paul says in 2 Corinthians 5:17 that once we start following Christ, we become "new creations." Who we once were is now gone. He has transformed us into something new. Something to remember, though, is that this heart change and transformation does not mean we are completely perfect the moment we start following Jesus. It just means our sins have been wiped away and God doesn't hold them against us. We have left the old things behind and started a new journey with Christ. We now have a future in front of us to allow Him to mold us into who He wants us to BE as we follow Him.

We can still choose to do the things we used to do instead of obeying Him. However, the blessing of learning to BE who God has called us to BE, is that we don't have to DO anything in our own power to change ourselves. We simply follow Him and BE who He has called us to be. We let Him change us. He brings us from death to life, putting a fresh purpose and hope inside of us that causes us to want to follow Him more. As we follow Him, letting Him change us, He brings us "from glory to glory," as Paul says in 2 Corinthians 3:18. This shows us that as we journey with Him, we will experience more and more of Him. As we experience Him, we are transformed.

FROM MILK TO MEAT

Something that I want to point out is that the transformation process should never stop for those who follow Jesus. However, there are specific, intentional seasons of change that God brings us through, individually. These seasons are different for everyone and affect us all uniquely.

These are seasons where God intentionally brings about a change in our lives in order to bring us to a greater level of spiritual maturity. It's the same principle as when a mother stops nursing her infant in order to give them more substantial food. This is a necessary point in the baby's development. The baby's instinct is to cry when they don't get the milk, but the change that needs to occur for them to grow properly is for them to learn to eat food. The same can be said of us as followers of Jesus. As we continue following Jesus, we must change from wanting just milk to wanting meat. God puts us through these seasons of change in order to wean us off of the milk of the word. We have to eat proper spiritual "food" in order for us to BE who He has called us to be. Paul emphasizes in Hebrews 5:12-14 "For though by this time you ought to be teachers, you need someone to teach you again the first principles of the oracles of God; and you have come to need milk and not solid food. For everyone who partakes only of milk is unskilled in the word of righteousness, for he is a babe. But solid food belongs to those who are of full age, that is, those who, by reason of use, have their senses exercised to discern both good and evil." In other words, there are those of us today who should be teachers of the gospel, but are stuck just drinking milk. They have consciously or unconsciously stopped maturing and changing. God uses seasons of change to mature us if we allow Him to. It's still our choice, though. We have the choice to keep being spiritual babies content with just milk. Or we can choose to grow up.

God wants to bring us through a season where He changes things in us so that we can eat the meat He offers. For some, this season can occur early in their spiritual development. They're ready for it, and God purposely plants them with people who will teach and disciple them. Others, though, might not be ready to give up the milk. They're content with where they are. In order to grow, they have to recognize where they are spiritually and allow themselves to change. Sometimes they refuse and stay stuck where they are, never growing. This kind of mentality is the breeding ground for complacency and can produce heresy and immorality. It is not pleasing to God. Even though the milk has its place in our spiritual formation, the only way for us to BE like Christ is when we desire and accept the meat He gives instead of settling only for the milk.

NEW WINE NEW WINESKINS

God also uses seasons of change to prepare us to experience a new, greater awareness of His glory and plan. Jesus said something that emphasizes this in Matthew 9:16-17.

> *"No one puts a piece of unshrunk cloth on an old garment; for the patch pulls away from the garment and the tear is made worse. Nor do they put new wine into old wineskins, or else the wineskins break, the wine is spilled, and the wineskins are ruined. But they put new wine into new wineskins, and both are preserved."*

Jesus was talking about how God wanted to do something new in His people to fulfill His plan of redemption. However, they could not handle what He was doing without being made new. We see the beginnings of this on the day of Pentecost, when the disciples were filled with the Holy Spirit. This was their season of change. Through Jesus, God made them suitable vessels to become His temple and were filled with the new wine of the Holy Spirit.

As the church grew after that day, we see God bring them through another season of change. He revealed that the Gentiles were a part of that plan of redemption as well. He wanted to bring the Gentiles into the family of God that already included the Israelites. They had to be willing to let go of their old biases and ways of thinking about the Gentiles in order for them to accept that. They had to become new wineskins to make way for what God was doing.

REVIVAL MEANS CHANGE

I believe that God is bringing the church into a season of growth the same way He did in Acts. He wants to reveal Himself in dramatic ways that will change us and those around us. However, it's going to require the church to go through a season of change and dying to the old ways of doing things.

We are always changing as we follow Jesus. The Holy Spirit reveals the truth of His word to us as we study it and seek to obey Him. We are changed by the power of the truth, and the Holy Spirit empowers us to live it out. Others around us are changed as well. A perfect example of this is in Acts 2. The disciples were filled with the Holy Spirit as they waited. Many people started following Jesus that day and in the weeks after that. The end of Acts 2 says that they grew in number and devoted themselves to the apostles' teachings. This implies that they were willing to learn something that they didn't know before. The result was that there was a genuine change in their hearts and lives. They sold their possessions in order to take care of their brothers and sisters in Christ, and to help the poor, the widow, and the orphan. Another example of this kind of transformation was in Peter. He went from a person who denied Christ three times out of fear just weeks before to boldly proclaiming that Jesus was the Messiah to all those gathered.

This is what a church who is open to genuine change looks like. New life occurs and people are set free from sin and follow Jesus wholeheartedly. These people change every day as they grow in the truth. However, when we don't follow the Holy Spirit and allow Him to transform us and reveal the truth to us, this change doesn't happen.

As a result, revival doesn't happen. People aren't set free. We become followers of rules or a false gospel instead of followers of

Jesus. To keep this point with the spirit of this book: We continue to DO things in our own power to bring the change we want. We have revival services and events to draw people in, but never experience true revival and heart change. We never get to where we learn to simply BE a follower of Jesus and let God be the one who changes us and those around us. He can grow His own kingdom. Those who continue to DO things in their own power instead of learning to BE His follower will destroy themselves, eventually.

There are two types of churches in America today that come to mind as I am talking about this. Before I go any further, keep in mind that I am not writing this to criticize and condemn these churches and the people that go to them in any way. Instead, my goal is to lovingly warn and correct, as a brother in Christ should, so that they can grow and change in a healthy, scriptural way.

- *DECAYING CHURCH*

The first image that comes to mind is a church building that is in decay and a congregation that is dying because of a lack of change. These churches have not gone outside of the four walls and tried to reach the surrounding society. They have not grown in numbers. As a result, they can't afford to take care of the building. Instead of developing discipleship and evangelism programs that reach the lost in this current generation, they are sitting in the church pew complaining about the changes in society and how it has become more and more corrupt. They spend all their church services saying that the end times are here and how much we need Jesus, but they do nothing to change what they are doing to reach people. They have lost the heart of Jesus for the lost. The heart that leaves the 99 to go after the 1.

Instead of building relationships with the lost like Jesus did and showing His love and speaking the truth, these churches pass out "gospel tracts" or yell at them that they are going to hell if they don't repent. This kind of "evangelism" shows that they've lost the understanding of what it means to make disciples and have replaced it with trying to make converts who say a "sinner's prayer." Converts don't truly experience true, lasting heart change. Disciples do. Let me just say something that might make some of you grab your steel-toed boots. There are a lot of churches that have this convert mentality instead of the heart of Jesus to make disciples. Some of you might have this mindset because that's the way you were taught. But, let me say this. This is lazy, selfish Christianity. This mindset is not pleasing to the heart of God that longs for people to know Him. He wants to reveal Himself to the broken and lost by sending us to them to bring them freedom. He reveals Himself by sending those who say "I will go," empowering them to do what He did and greater things. We are His ambassadors sent to a lost and dying world. If ambassadors didn't live among the people and represent the kingdom they were sent from, they would be pointless. It's sad that this is an illustration of a lot of churches in America today. They DO a lot of things in the name of Jesus, but aren't truly being the ambassadors they are called to BE as His followers. They have stopped allowing the Holy Spirit to transform and use them and are dying.

- *COMPLACENT CHURCH*

The second image that comes to mind is a beautiful, enormous church building. This church has an amazing worship team, amazing children's program, and a feeding program for the poor in the city. This kind of church appears to have everything together. On the inside, however, they are dying from a lack of change just as much as the church that is actually dying from a lack of numbers. Instead of teaching and expounding on the word of God fully, pastors have preached their opinions or have allowed emotions to cloud and distort the truth. They preach tolerance and happy, self-help messages instead of preaching on sin and judgment because they don't want to offend anyone.

A lot of Charismatic/Pentecostal churches today are led more by emotional experiences rather than sound teaching. I come from a charismatic background and have seen this firsthand. Some of these churches rely more on feelings and "goosebumps" to determine what the Holy Spirit is doing. As a result, there are things happening that are completely against scripture. On the other side of the spectrum, a lot of more traditional churches don't teach about experiencing the Holy Spirit and being empowered by Him at all. They teach that God doesn't move like that anymore.

In both cases, truth from scripture and learning to follow the Holy Spirit correctly have been neglected. As a result, true heart change and revival have stopped and these churches are dying spiritually. This is a perfect example of what it means to quench the Holy Spirit. I believe with all of my heart that this grieves His heart. He wants to move in power and reveal truth to those who are hungry to know Him. He wants to bring true revival that changes the hearts of people, not "feel-good" experiences. If the leaders of these churches are not willing to make the changes necessary, He will not move, no matter how much we ask Him to.

SALT AND LIGHT

Again, I'm not saying these things about these churches to be judgmental and condemning towards those who are part of them. I am saying this because God wants to bring transformation. Revival can't happen if the people who make up His body are not changing first and becoming more like Christ. Unfortunately, these two types of churches are an illustration of the American church. We have stopped BEING like Christ in favor of DOING our own thing. As a result, the church is looking more and more like the world. This is not how God intended us to be. We are called to be salt and light to the world. We cannot do this if we have lost our flavor and stopped allowing Christ to shine through us.

If we are not allowing the Holy Spirit to transform us into the church He wants us to BE, then there will be no revival, no matter how many prayer meetings we hold. There will be no change in the world. If we do not become like Him and let Him continually transform us in order to be better witnesses to the world around us, we will be flavorless and useless.

WINDS OF CHANGE

The same can be said of us as individuals who make up the church. Are we allowing ourselves to be planted in a season of change or are we resisting change? Is there new life coming up in and from us, or are we stuck in the same old ways of doing things?

God gave me a vision a few months ago about this very thing that is a prophetic message about where we are as a church and what He wants to do. He showed me a picture of a desert with an oasis in the middle of it. There was a wall surrounding it. Then, I saw that a wind came and blew the walls down. The oasis spread into the desert, bringing new life to the sands.

The meaning of this vision is this: the church is the oasis. The world is the desert. God had brought us to life in the middle of a dead world with a purpose to spread into the desert and bring it back to life. Instead of spreading, though, we built a wall around us to keep the desert from coming in. We were comfortable inside of those walls and had become useless.

However, God showed me that He is about to bring us into a season that will bring us back to our original purpose. He said that He was sending a wind of change to break down the walls of comfort we built so that we would spread into the dead world and bring it back to life again. He showed me that some would be resistant to this change because they are comfortable where they are. There will also be resistance from the harsh environment of the desert world. He said that if the church pushes through the resistance and embraces the changes, there would be revival again and we would see new life.

NECESSARY CHANGES

So what changes do you need to make to experience growth? It might be a lifestyle of sin, or maybe you just aren't willing to let go of your comfortable lifestyle in order to follow Jesus. God wants for us to experience the depths of who He is and become more like Him in every way. We have to allow Him to lead us through those changes and transform us so that we can BE like Christ. Only when these changes occur can we grow the Kingdom of God and bring new life to this world.

My prayer is this. God let the winds of change come and destroy the walls separating us from growth. Transform us so that we can stop DOING things apart from you and instead BE like you. Lead us to those who need change as well to bring your freedom to a lost and dying world. I hope this is your prayer too.

CHAPTER 7
SEASONS OF PAIN

J esus tells us in Matthew 16:24-26

> *"If anyone desires to come after Me, let him deny*
> *himself, and take up his cross, and follow Me.*
> *For whoever desires to save his life will lose it,*
> *but whoever loses his life for My sake will find it.*
> *For what profit is it to a man if he gains the*
> *whole world, and loses his own soul? Or what*
> *will a man give in exchange for his soul?"*

Over two thousand years later, we know that Jesus was crucified on a cross. We also know that crucifixion is one of the most painful ways to die. In this statement, Jesus was foreshadowing His own death on the cross and saying that following Him would require us to lay down our own safety and comfort for the sake of the gospel. As followers of Jesus, carrying the cross means that we will always experience pain and even death as we follow Him. However, this pain is a part of the growth process and helps us to BE like Christ.

We die to ourselves and endure the pain so that we can live free in Him. If Christ can endure the pain of the cross, then we can endure pain as well.

There are two types of pain: pain from suffering and the pain of growth. The pain that comes from suffering is involuntary. The pain that comes from growth is voluntary. As we follow Him, He will lead us through seasons where we will experience these types of pain. While we are experiencing this pain it is important to remember that He is good, His plan is good, and He is with us.

GOD'S PLAN

If you've served Jesus for a while, you've probably heard this question. "How can a good God who loves us so much allow so much pain in the world?" This question is the reason many people choose not to follow God. There are some who say that pain is a part of God's plan. I disagree with this teaching. Yes, God uses pain to accomplish a purpose. However, pain was never God's plan for us. It's not in His nature to cause harm to His creation. However, there is an enemy, Satan, whose goal is to "kill, steal, and destroy" as Jesus says in John 10:10. He will do whatever he can to cause pain and destruction and keep us from being who God wants us to be. It's important for us to remember this and remember who God is as we go through seasons of pain.

GOD IS GOOD

Scripture tells us that God is wholly and completely good. Evil cannot exist within or around Him. It also says in Jeremiah 29:11 that His plans for us are good and His thoughts are thoughts of peace and plans to give us a future and hope with Him. In the original Hebrew that the Old Testament was written in, the word peace in this passage is the word "*shalom*" which means completeness and wholeness, implying that God's plan is for us to be completely whole in every aspect of life. We know now, centuries after Jeremiah prophesied this verse, that He brought this plan to fruition through Jesus' sacrifice and through the empowerment of the Holy Spirit. So for God to be the one to cause death and suffering as part of His plan would contradict that and would take away from His character.

PERFECT CREATION

But what about natural disasters or diseases that cause people to suffer? If God is good and in control of nature, couldn't He just stop natural disasters and disease from happening? The answer is yes, He could. He could step in and change things for the better for every person everywhere. The problem with Him doing that is this: In Genesis, when God created the heavens and the earth, it was perfect. No natural disasters, no disease, no sickness, etc. When He created the first man and woman, Adam and Eve, He gave them dominion over all the earth to rule. But, when they disobeyed God and ate the fruit that He had forbidden them to eat, they gave their authority to Satan. That's when evil entered the world through sin and death and the world became corrupted by that evil causing the natural disasters we see today.

It was never God's plan for this to happen. God's plan was for creation to be perfect and for us to rule it with Him. God doesn't force us to obey this plan, though. He gave Adam a choice. So, when Adam gave his authority away to Satan, the only way for God to step in and change things would be if we ask for it. That's why prayer is so important. We are interceding on behalf of others when we ask God to intervene.

I think it's important to note that just because God allows pain; it doesn't mean that He doesn't have a plan to end it. We see in John 3:16 that God loved the world so much that He sent His Son Jesus to die to redeem it. The original word used in this verse is the Greek word *Kosmos,* which is also translated as the word "universe." So what this verse is saying is that God loved the universe or the entire creation so much that His plan was to send Jesus so that He could see it redeemed and made new again.

It is also important to note that because the entire universe has fallen because of the corruption of sin, in order for Him to stop natural disasters, He would have to demolish the world and make something new that is perfect again. That is His plan, though, as we see prophesied in Revelation.

MERCY NOT JUDGMENT

I know that there are those who will argue that God is a hateful God who causes suffering. There are passages of scripture where God talks about raining death and destruction down upon nations. This, of course, causes pain. But, if you look at the context of these scriptures, every one of them is pointing to this kind of suffering being judgment or justice because of the sins and evil actions of the specific nation. They are also always given a warning that this judgment will happen in the future if they don't repent and if they do, God will have mercy. This shows that it is always part of God's plan to have mercy, not judgment. It is the nation's or individual's choice to keep going down the path that leads to their judgment and destruction.

THE REASON FOR PAIN

As I mentioned earlier, there are two types of pain: involuntary pain that comes with suffering and voluntary pain that comes with growth. Suffering happens to everyone at some point and comes as the involuntary loss of something. It could be the involuntary loss of friendships or family through division or death. Also, it could be the loss of wealth, status, or popularity because of a choice to follow God. It could also be the loss of safety and comfort because of abuse or violence directed at you. Suffering is hard no matter how it comes. The person going through it will experience some kind of emotional, mental, or physical pain and turmoil.

Growing pains, however, occur when we experience growth. It's implied in the name. Growth requires pain to be true growth. Where pain from suffering is involuntary, pain from growth is completely voluntary. This means you have the choice to endure the pain that comes from growth and submit to God as He brings you through the process.

So why does a good God allow so much pain? Why can't He just cause us all to be perfect and not experience suffering or growing pains? There is an answer that Christians like to give when asked this question. "God's ways are higher than our ways." I want to submit to you that this statement isn't the answer people need to hear during painful seasons. Yes, this is a true statement that's straight from Scripture. God's ways are higher than ours. We can't understand His reasons for doing things sometimes. However, people don't want to hear this. They want reasons for why we suffer. They want suffering to end. Unfortunately, pain will never go away because we live in a fallen world. However, God does have reasons why He brings us through seasons of pain. Reasons that, if we focus on them, will help us thrive through the seasons of pain. There are two very clear ones. To refine us into the people He wants us to BE and to show His glory and power.

1. THE REFINERS FIRE

God allows suffering to refine us. The word refine means to remove impurities. When God refines us by allowing us to go through suffering, He is removing the weakness and impurities from us so that we can become perfect. Those who endure through suffering with a positive mentality will come out stronger than before. Especially if they put their trust in God through the pain of suffering, knowing that He will see them through it and work everything out for their good and benefit. These kinds of people are those who, even though they might have lost everything, maintain a healthy outlook on life and are "rich in spirit." They live at peace, love the most, are the kindest, most gentle, and generous people on the earth. Just like gold, those who have been brought through the fire of suffering come out purified and perfect.

There is a story in the Bible that emphasizes this in the book of Job. Job was a wealthy man who served God faithfully. The devil, or Satan as we also know him, saw this and challenged God, saying that if He took His protection away from Job, then he would reject Him. God agreed and removed His protection, allowing Satan to bring suffering to Job. Job lost everything within days. His servants were killed by the Sabeans, his livestock were stolen by the Chaldeans or killed by fire from heaven. His house was destroyed as well, by a great wind, killing his children inside of it. But, despite all this destruction and loss, Job's response was to worship God. After that, Satan took it further by attacking Jobs' health. He put boils on his skin, causing him great pain. It got to where even Job's wife told him to curse God and die. Through it all, Job remained faithful to God. Because of this, after all the pain and suffering ended, God blessed Job and gave him twice as much as he had before.

NO PAIN NO GAIN

God also uses the pain that comes from growth to refine us. If you've been around people who exercise long enough, you've probably heard the phrase "no pain, no gain." What these people are saying is that the only way to achieve the physical change you want to see is when you push your body beyond its limits. You work to get rid of or add whatever it is you're wanting to change about your physical appearance. Some people do it for good reasons like health issues or to lose weight. Others do it out of insecurities and social pressure to look a certain way. Whatever the reason, people who work out and exercise experience pain in order to achieve the results they want. Weightlifters and bodybuilders exert themselves, increasing the amount of weight they lift in order to push their muscles beyond their limits. Runners train their bodies to run longer distances, pushing their legs and lungs to go further and further. Athletes train in their sport to get better and get rid of bad habits and techniques. All of them experience pain along the way. But when they reach their goals and their bodies get used to the exertion, the pain decreases. When this happens, they set new goals and begin new training to push their bodies further.

In my experience with working out, I know for a fact it hurts, especially at first because my body isn't used to the exertion I'm putting it through. My muscles are always sore for days afterwards until they become used to the exertion I'm putting them through. As my body becomes used to what I am doing, it hurts less and less. This shows growth in strength and endurance. I then have the choice to set new goals and grow further, just keep doing what I am doing, or even give up because the pain is too great. If I am consistent with working out, I see results in my health, endurance, and weight. However, if I don't stay consistent and stop working out after a while, I lose all of what I have gained.

The same can be said of those who follow Jesus as we learn how to BE like Him. He never promised that it would be easy. The statement "take up your cross and follow me" implies that the cross will be heavy. As you walk with Him and allow Him to transform, you might get tired and might feel pain. But, just as the results of working out make it worth the pain, the hope and freedom we have as we grow in Him are worth the pain and suffering we will go through.

SANCTIFICATION

To put it in Biblical "churchy" terms, the growth process of a follower of Jesus is the process of sanctification. Sanctification is the work that the Holy Spirit does in us to purify us and make us holy. It is a lifelong process and requires us to die to ourselves and our fleshly desires as He does the work of pruning us in order to clean out what doesn't belong and tempering us so that we can truly live free to become who He has called us to be. While sanctification might not bring physical pain, it will bring emotional pain that we will have to learn how to deal with as we learn to BE more like Jesus.

EMOTIONAL PAIN

Anyone who has ever had negative emotions knows that they are not fun to experience. They are very uncomfortable and even painful to go through. In fact, because of our culture, the average American spends more effort trying to escape emotional pain rather than confront it in a healthy way. We have cell phones that distract us from whatever negative emotions we are feeling or even feed them if that's what we want. We have alcohol that we drink to escape the pain, as well as drugs that our therapists prescribe if we're depressed or anxious. Addictions can result from someone trying to escape pain. For most Americans, the way to escape from emotional pain is just to stay busy with whatever distracts them.

For followers of Jesus, there are several kinds of emotional pain that we can experience during the growth process. Most of you will have experienced this discomfort at some point in your walk with Christ. Some of you might even be experiencing it now. I want to take this time to stress that you are not alone in this. Jesus Himself went through moments of stress where He had to make a choice of whether He was going to give in to the pain of it or not. He chose not to. We are experiencing the results of His endurance 2000 years later. Here are some examples of emotional stress and discomfort that all followers of Jesus will experience at some point.

- *Guilt and Shame*

This pain might come as frustration or guilt and shame from mistakes we make. Even though we want to be perfect, we still mess up. When we inevitably mess up, it feels like we just can't get it right and will never be who God wants us to be. From my experience, these thoughts are painful. I am a perfectionist and set high standards for myself. When I don't meet these standards and make mistakes, I feel embarrassment, anger, and frustration at myself. For a moment, I believe the lie that I can never overcome whatever it is I'm struggling with. I know that there are others who are like this as well. For some, these thoughts and feelings lead to depression and even suicidal thoughts if they are not dealt with and brought under control.

As we grow and learn to BE like Jesus, the Holy Spirit will remind us of the truth. He has set us free. Nothing can change this. He is faithful to forgive us and give us the grace we need to get back up. We don't need to let guilt and shame keep us from growing. The only way to push past these negative emotions is to learn to focus only on this truth. I will talk more about our focus in a later chapter.

- *Temptation*

Every follower of Jesus experiences temptation that can come with a lot of negative emotions. Temptations come in situations where we have to choose whether to obey our flesh or obey the Holy

Spirit. These situations will most likely come with a level of emotional and maybe even physical pain.

An example of this could be a quarrel with an enemy where you had to choose how to react. Before giving your life to Christ and beginning the process of sanctification, you might have reacted with violence or verbally assaulting them. While the anger might still be there as a temptation, you have the choice to react like you used to or to choose not to fight. Controlling anger when you're used to giving into it might be stressful. Our natural instinct might be to give in to the flesh, but the growth that comes from self-control is worth going through the stress. Yes, there could be pain that comes from their verbal or physical attacks if the other person reacts violently. But as you grow, even the anger will eventually dissolve because you will learn to have perfect peace in His presence even during chaos, conflict, and even violence.

Another example of a make or break situation that might hit home for some of us, especially men, is sexual temptation. Because we are created to be sexual creatures, resisting sexual temptation can be really hard. It can be very easy to give in to the pleasure in the moment, especially if you aren't used to resisting it. The pain can come from having to give up the pleasure you feel. It's hard because you want it so badly that giving it up feels like giving up something good. But, because of what we read in scripture, we know that sexual intercourse before marriage is sin. The consequences are not worth the pleasure we experience. The growth that we experience when we use self-control is worth the pain of resisting the pleasure. Self-control leads to greater growth and blessings in the future. Statistics show that marriages are stronger and healthier when both individuals involved choose to be abstinent before and during that relationship. It's worth the wait.

- *Fear, Worry, Doubt, and Confusion*

As we progress in our relationship with Jesus, the Holy Spirit teaches us to rest and trust in Him. As we progress, though, especially in the beginning stages, there will be moments when we experience negative emotions such as fear, worry, doubt, and confusion. These emotions could distract us from resting and trusting in Him if we aren't careful. Focusing on them will cause us great pain and could even jeopardize our journey to becoming like Christ if we don't learn how to push through them.

I know there are several things that can cause these emotions for even the strongest follower of Jesus. The biggest one is probably finances. From experience, in the moment of not being able to pay your rent or bills, the emotional pain that comes from worrying about how you are going to pay them can seem so overwhelming. Because of this worry, we take our eyes off of Jesus and put them on the problem. Doing this causes the problem to seem bigger than Jesus is. We forget what Scripture says about how God will provide, how God has helped and provided in the past, and we question whether or not He will provide. If we are not careful, we can stop trusting in God completely and take matters in our own hands, getting further and further into debt from credit cards and loans, or even resorting to stealing. As we mature through the process of sanctification, this worry will become easier to recognize as a lie. Once we recognize the lie, we can push through it, resting in the truth of who God is, and trusting that He will take care of our needs if we obey Him.

These emotions can also affect our prayer life and, as a result, our relationship with God. Instead of praying bold prayers with our requests and needs, we question whether or not God hears us, causing us to not even pray at all or not praying for what we are asking for. Sometimes God will not answer because we didn't even ask Him. As we mature in our relationship with Him, we will see His faithfulness and grow in praying with boldness. Rather than being controlled by worry, fear, and doubt and questioning whether someone will be healed when we pray for them or not, instead we lay hands on them and pray in boldness and authority. We remember in that moment that God has promised to heal when we pray for the sick.

The same can be said of how we approach the Great Commission in Mark 16:15-18. Jesus commands us to go into all the world and preach the gospel. He then promises that certain things would happen as we follow and obey Him. Fear, doubt, worry and confusion will creep up in order to distract us from this calling. We will sometimes worry or be afraid of what people around us will think if we talk about Jesus to them. We might even be afraid of being attacked or put to death for this, depending on where we live in the world. However, as we mature in our relationship with Jesus, He will empower us through His Holy Spirit. He will give us the boldness we need to push past the initial pain of worry, doubt, and fear that we will experience. Lives will change when we obey His command to go preach the gospel. We even see people leaving everything behind in order to go to another part of the world to obey this command.

- *Loss*

Following Jesus can result in loss as well. Loss is very painful. While this is also suffering, the difference between the suffering I mentioned at the beginning of the chapter is that the pain that comes because of loss for the sake of Christ is voluntary. The choice is yours to follow Christ and accept the losses that come with it. It is possible that you will lose friends and family members who reject you because of your decision to follow Christ. You will sacrifice dreams you had in order to follow the calling and purpose He has given you. You might lose status or a career because you choose to follow Christ. Some of us might even lose our lives because we choose to obey the Great Commission and preach the gospel.

However, for each loss, you will gain something far greater as you grow in Christ. You will gain a Father who will never fail or leave you, a Friend who sticks closer than a brother. You will gain a family of like-minded people who follow Jesus who will stick with you, encouraging you and building you up even during pain. Also, you will gain a purpose and a calling that is greater than any career or dream you might have had. Finally, you will gain perfection and eternity with God.

2. OUR GOOD HIS GLORY

The second reason I believe God brings us through seasons of pain is so that He can get the glory when He supernaturally turns the situation around. So many times in the Bible, we see God's people suffering. Then God steps in and delivers them, reversing the situation. When this happens, people's hearts and lives are changed. God uses suffering not only to strengthen and purify the people going through it, but also to use them to grow His kingdom and deliver others around them.

We see this in the book of Acts with the example of the church as it was beginning. They were suffering at the hands of the religious leaders in Jerusalem and the Gentiles, being put to death for their faith in Jesus. But, because of the faith of the followers of Jesus and the empowerment of the Holy Spirit, this persecution had the opposite result than the enemy intended. Instead of this new movement being put down by pain and suffering, it actually grew. People around the believers saw them being delivered regularly. One example was when Peter was set free from prison by an angel in Acts 12. Another example was when Paul and Silas were miraculously set free from prison in Acts 16. An earthquake caused by God had broken open the cell while they were praising Jesus. In each of these instances, people saw these miraculous deliverances and responded by choosing to follow Jesus as well.

We also see this demonstrated in the story of Joseph in Genesis. Joseph was the favorite son of Jacob. His other brothers were jealous of him, so they sold him into slavery. He ended up in Egypt as the slave of the captain of Pharoahs guard, Potiphar. While in slavery, Joseph was made head of Potiphar's house because of his wisdom and character, until one day Potiphar's wife tried to get him to sleep with her. He ran from her, but she lied to Potiphar, saying that he tried to rape her, so he was thrown into prison. God used him to interpret two of Pharaoh's servants' dreams while in prison. Later, he was brought before Pharaoh himself to interpret his dreams. The dream's meaning was that there would be seven years of plenty followed by seven years of famine. Because of this interpretation, Pharaoh saw God's wisdom in Joseph and made him the governor over all of Egypt, second only to him. Joseph spent the next seven years of plenty preparing for the seven years of famine. When that time came, people came from all over the region to buy food from Egypt. Joseph's brothers came to buy food as well. The second time they came, he revealed himself to them. They repented and his whole family moved to Egypt so that he could care for them. There is a famous line spoken by Joseph to his brothers in Genesis 50 in response to their fear that he would kill them.

> *"But as for you, you meant evil against me; but God meant it for good, in order to bring it about as it is this day, to save many people alive."*

Because Joseph remained faithful to God through his suffering, He turned the entire situation around in order to save the entire region from starvation.

YOU CAN DO IT

My encouragement to those who are experiencing pain right now, whether voluntary or involuntary, is this: You can endure the pain. Yes, it will be hard and there will be times where you might feel like giving up, but you can do it. One thing to remember through pain and discomfort is that, even when it doesn't feel like it, you are not alone. Take comfort in the truth that God is with you and that there are thousands of people who are praying for people just like you. Don't let pain break you and keep you from growing. Don't get stuck in a cycle of trying to DO things to escape your pain, either. Endure the pain and BE the follower of Jesus you are called to be. Rest in Him. Let Him comfort you through it instead of turning to other things to numb the pain. If you need it and can get it, get help from people such as coaches, pastors, and counselors who work in mental and spiritual health. Take advantage of these people. They are available to help guide people through times of pain. Find friends who will walk with you and encourage you through suffering. Even if it feels like you can't, stay positive and obedient through it, realizing that the end is near and you'll emerge victorious and strong. God's promise in Scripture is that He will turn all tears into laughter, all sorrow into joy, and all mourning into dancing. There will be no more pain. Only perfect joy and peace. He is faithful, good, and promises to work all things for your good.

CHAPTER 8
SEASONS OF PREPARATION

Have you ever had a dream or desire that just always seems so far out of reach? Or a goal you have that no matter how hard you work towards it, you can't seem to achieve it? How many of us have stayed up late crying out to God about the things we want Him to do? If you're a human like me, you've probably experienced this once or twice, or a hundred times. Just this week I've experienced the frustration of having a desire that once again seems to feel so far off. In fact, I'm feeling it right now as I'm writing this if I'm being honest.

DREAMS VERSUS REALITY

Welcome to your season of preparation; the space between dreams fulfilled and the reality of where you are right now in life. Here, you will experience moments of frustration, heartache, anxiety, anger, bitterness, depression, sadness, confusion, loneliness, and other negative emotions. One minute, you might feel like you're winning, getting ahead, and accomplishing great things. The next minute, though, something can happen that shows you just how far you are from the goal. My friends, let me encourage you with this. This space and season can be one of significant growth, peace, and joy. It all depends on how you choose to view the season or situation you're in. Your perspective will determine how you handle the tension between dreams and reality. It also determines what kind of person you will be when the season is over.

You've probably heard it a thousand or even a million times that God has a plan. If it's meant to happen, it'll happen. This saying sounds good, but is actually not completely true. It might even cause people to focus on unrealistic dreams and miss out on what God actually wants to do. Yes, I completely believe that God has a plan and a purpose for our lives. However, I also believe that we have a choice to pursue God's plan or not. In the space between dreams and the reality of where we are at now, there is a choice. A choice to continue to pursue our own dreams or His. A choice to allow our emotions to remove us from the path God has us on. There is a choice to trust God to lead and open doors in His timing. A choice to give up and start chasing our own easier dreams. We have a choice to keep on DOING things that don't matter or to BE followers of Jesus. We also have the choice to adapt and let Him be the one to do the work in and through us. Part of the season of preparation is learning patience and how to wait on God so that we can see the dream He has put on our hearts fulfilled.

THE PRACTICE OF WAITING

Anyone who struggles with patience or has a short attention span will agree that it takes a lot of self-control to wait. So how do we change that in order to develop a habit of waiting for God? And what does waiting on God even mean?

There are two scriptures in particular that I want to use in order to define the word "wait": Psalm 27:14 and Isaiah 40:31. Both scriptures say to wait on the Lord in order to gain strength. The original Hebrew word used in both scriptures is the word "*qavah*" which means to look to, to hope in, and to expect. It also has an action attached to it, meaning to minister to or serve. This is where we get the words "waiter" or "waitress" from. This shows us that we are to look to Jesus, hoping in Him, and expecting Him to fulfill the promises He has for us. We also wait for Him to change us and our situations for His glory, giving us strength and endurance. While we do that, we serve Him faithfully and obediently, ministering to Him with our prayers, praise, and acts of worship through obedience and servanthood. (If any of you who are reading this are like me at all, reading these verses this way probably blows your mind just as much as it did mine. I love how deep scripture can be.)

Waiting takes a lot of practice and self-control, which is why it's a spiritual discipline that we must master during the season of preparation God has us in. As we learn to rest in Him, we also learn to let go of DOING things that distract us. Unfortunately, followers of Jesus in today's society, especially Americans, are out of practice in the spiritual discipline of waiting. We want what we want when we want it. We chase after our own desires and settle for lesser things that aren't God's best. When we are afraid or stressed, we give up because we feel like we can't handle it anymore. However, when we cultivate a mindset of waiting on God in our daily habits and ways of thinking, we start to wait naturally. Instead of giving up and giving in to depression and anxiety, we learn to wait for Him to move in our battles, storms, and trials. We wait on Him to open the right doors in His timing instead of forcing doors open ourselves. We don't just sit there talking to Him and not actually listening to what He's saying and doing. When we pray, we wait for him to speak to us. We wait on Him to give us the desires of our hearts and the answers to our prayers because we know He has the best for us. We stop DOING and learn to just BE. As we follow and wait on Him, He renews our strength just like Isaiah says.

HE RENEWS

To put it practically, my challenge to you is this. Look at an area of your life that you are praying that God will move in. It could be a situation at work, sin struggle, relationship issue, financial burden, or just wanting to grow closer to God. Now think of it this way. How are you waiting on God in prayer for the situation? Are you giving into your negative emotions about this issue and giving up? Or are you resting in God, allowing Him to give you peace and waiting for Him to change it? Are you serving Him willingly and obediently while you're waiting? If the answer is no, my challenge for you is to begin with spending a few moments in reflection on this and examining your own heart. Then ask God to help you wait on Him. After that, build the habit of spending a few moments each day praying scripture and His promises over the issue. When you feel down, shift your focus from the problem to Him. A way to help focus on this is to journal and write the dates that you prayed, and see how your perspective shifts each day. He is the answer and has all the answers to all the questions and challenges.

When we wait on the Lord, He renews our strength. We can then mount on the wings of eagles and soar above the problems. We can run the race set before us and not grow weary. For this to be reality we must learn to develop the discipline of waiting in order to become the people He has called us to be.

ENCOURAGE YOURSELF

David is the perfect example from Scripture of waiting for God's promise to come to fruition. David had been anointed king of Israel by Samuel after Saul had disobeyed God in 1 Samuel 15. However, he had to wait for years before the time that he was crowned king came. During that season of waiting and preparation, he served Saul and was obedient to God. God gave him great favor with the people and was with Him. Scripture tells us that David encouraged himself in the Lord whenever he was feeling down. The lesson that we can learn from David is that while we are waiting on the promise of God to come, we must serve where we are placed, and learn to encourage ourselves in the Lord.

PRUNING

Another thing that God has taught me in the last few years is this. Sometimes our dreams haven't become reality because they aren't the dreams He's given us. So, in the space between the dream and reality, He prunes the things that don't belong. During the season of preparation, He reshapes our dreams and goals into what He wants for us if we allow Him to.

In gardening, pruning is cutting back the parts of a plant or tree that are dead or hinder it from growing further or producing fruit. This process helps the plant or tree grow and produce better fruit. This process occurs for a believer as well. If we submit to the Holy Spirit's leading, He will bring us through a pruning season. The parts of us that are actually hindering our growth and the growth of others are cut off. Only then can we become who He has called us to BE.

There are many ways this process can occur in our lives. For some, it might just be bad mindsets or opinions that need to be pruned to make way for truth and God's wisdom. For others, it can be habits and lifestyles such as watching shows on Netflix or listening to music that might be slightly inappropriate. These might not necessarily be bad, but aren't leading to growth, so they have to be removed. For many others, it might be sinful habits that they haven't dealt with or been convicted of. It might even be dreams and plans that might come from motives to serve God, but aren't what God fully wants. Whatever the case may be, God wants the best for His people and sometimes it means getting rid of the old to make way for the new. He does this through pruning.

Let me give you two perfect examples from my own life. The first was my season of singleness. Before the woman that God had for me came along, I spent years wanting and praying for a beautiful wife who loves and follows Jesus. Someone I can grow with, have fun with, have deep talks with and the next minute start laughing hysterically at some random nonsense. Thankfully, God eventually answered this prayer and brought someone into my life that I adore. My reality, though, was that before she came along, I was thirty-three years old and still single. There was a tension in the space between my singleness and desire to be married. A space and a season that came with a lot of moments of emotions, both positive and negative, depending on my perspective. I was tempted and distracted from waiting for God during this season. I'm not going to lie; I sometimes gave into those distractions and got into relation-ships that I knew I wasn't supposed to be in. I knew these girls were wrong for me, but I dated them anyway because I was lonely and emotionally unhealthy. I didn't want to admit it to myself, though.

Fortunately, when someone truly desires to follow God, He is always faithful to get us back on track. Sometimes He protects us from ourselves. In my case, He protected me by removing those women from my life. He also taught me a lesson in self-awareness and self-control so that I could recognize and overcome my bad habits and mindset. Once I gained an awareness of my need to become emotionally healthy, I started recognizing things in myself that He was pruning and molding in this season of preparation. My mindset about my singleness changed, and I started appreciating what God was doing in this season. I started thanking Him for my singleness and for teaching me to be content. I also asked for Him to teach me to depend on Him to bring me the one He wanted me to marry because I wanted to wait on Him, instead of taking my dating life into my own hands. This was when I realized I was in a season of preparation. God was trying to prune unhealthy desires that I had in order to make me into a man who was ready to marry the one He had for me. So I submitted to this process and grew. Then one day, He brought the perfect person into my life. The waiting and preparation paid off.

I want to use another example from my own life to emphasize how God prunes. Some of you in ministry might relate to this story. A few years ago, I went through a three year pruning season. After college, I worked for a campus ministry called Chi Alpha for three years. After my second year, I felt the calling to move to Louisville, Kentucky. Because I was still doing college ministry at the time, I thought it was to pioneer a new Chi Alpha. So I moved back to Kentucky to pursue this dream.

I felt strongly about this calling and wanted people to support me. However, there were several barriers that ultimately showed me that God was not in this calling. The first was finances. As a missionary I was required to raise my own support. However, I was never able to raise the financial support that I needed to continue working for Chi Alpha. The second was that the state leadership did not want a Chi Alpha at U of L at that time. So, after a conversation with the Chi Alpha state director, I stepped back from Chi Alpha. Despite this, I still knew that God wanted me to be in Louisville. Believing this as well, a pastor friend offered me a volunteer position at his church serving as the young adult pastor. I accepted it and moved to Louisville. However, I still had not let go of the dream to plant a Chi Alpha at U of L.

I served there for three years, all the while waiting for God to show me if He still wanted me to plant a Chi Alpha at U of L or not. During those three years, I slowly realized that I had to let the dream of pioneering die. Honestly, it was very difficult because that dream and passion to reach college students had become part of my identity. I refused to give it up. Honestly, my stubbornness made this season harder than it needed to be. I was miserable and continued to go around in circles, making foolish decisions, trying to alleviate the frustration I was feeling. Some of you might be in similar situations and can relate. Fortunately, after months of frustration, I finally recognized what God was trying to do. He was pruning my desires in order to make way for His will to be done.

During this process and season of pruning, God reminded me of other dreams I had forgotten about. He showed me that I had not allowed myself to pursue them because I was focused on the dream of reaching college students and pioneering a Chi Alpha. I was so focused on DOING the work of ministry to college students that I had not learned to just BE His follower. I had also not grown in my giftings that He had given me. As a result, I was incomplete and miserable. I repented and in the following months, God reshaped my mindsets and instilled a new vision inside of me. He challenged me to use my giftings to grow His kingdom. One of them was writing. It was out of this season of pruning and preparation that this book was conceived.

Pruning can be a long, painful process. However, if we allow Him to prune the old ways of DOING things, He will also teach us how to simply BE like Christ.

DISCERNMENT

I learned a valuable lesson in these experiences. It's during these seasons of preparation that the enemy comes in the most to distract us from learning whatever God is trying to teach us. Therefore, it is so important to grow in discernment so that we can recognize these distractions for what they are: attempts by the enemy to keep us from growing. He knows our weaknesses and seeks to use them against us in order to keep us from learning to BE like Christ.

Let me give a few real-life examples of what this looks like. I'm sure most of you will identify with at least one or two of these.

GOOD VERSUS GOD

One way that the enemy distracts us is by putting things that look good in our path. While they might not be bad things, the problem is that they are not God's best and we must recognize the difference.

A good example of this is dating. Dating is hard, especially as a single follower of Jesus who is trying to live life pure and holy before marriage in today's overly sexual culture. Most Christian singles set standards for themselves and have specific character traits that they look and pray for in a mate. They pray for God to bring this perfect person into their lives that they can fall in love with and marry. Unfortunately, more and more Christian singles today are distracted from that standard and settling for second best. I am a perfect example of this, as I mentioned earlier in this chapter. While the girls I dated weren't bad girls who led me into sin, they weren't God's best for me. I was distracted from what God wanted for me when I chose to pursue them. Fortunately, God protected me by ending those relationships and removing most of them from my life. Yes, it was painful, but necessary.

Unfortunately, I know several people whose stories had a different outcome. I know people who used to be in successful ministries but their new spouse didn't want to be in ministry and influenced their decision to leave. I know several people who aren't even followers of Jesus anymore because they married someone who wasn't a Christian. Paul tells us in 2 Corinthians 2:1 not to be unequally yoked with an unbeliever. This is especially important because of the dangers of getting distracted from growing in your faith. I will take it a step further by saying that no one should get into a relationship with someone who is not willing to support you in your calling. You also shouldn't be with someone who does not share your core beliefs and practices or someone who isn't at the same spiritual hunger level as you. It will be much harder to stay focused on your own growth and growing the relationship with Christ at the center.

I use this example because being single is a hard season, especially as you get older, and it's easy to become distracted. I'm speaking from experience and I know most of you who are single will relate to me. My challenge is that we should all view singleness as a season of preparation. God has us in this season to prepare us for marriage and whatever else He has for us. I've heard this quote spoken before; I'm not sure from where, so I can't quote the author. A lot of you might have heard it before as well. "Become who you want to marry." This quote is very true and applicable. If you want to marry a person who loves Jesus and lives for Him, then become someone who loves Him and lives for Him with everything you are. If you want someone who helps others and challenges them to be the best they can, become someone who helps and challenges others. The list can go on. You know what you want. Add whatever you're looking for to that list. The most important goal is to learn to BE like Jesus. With the power and purification of the Holy Spirit, learn to BE like Him while you are single, so that you can attract the best mate who is also like Him. Never settle for less and keep asking God to give you the desires of your heart or to change your desires through pruning, if that's what He wants. Ask Him for discernment to know what's right for you or not. Serve Him while you are waiting. Let Him be the one to mold you into who He wants you to be for your future spouse and pray that He molds him/her as well.

The same can be said of careers. There are times where we might have good ideas and dreams that seem to be from God, but are not from God at all. They could be manifestations of our own desires that haven't been surrendered to God or distractions set in our path by the enemy. My story about how I thought I was supposed to plant a college ministry at University of Louisville is a perfect example of this. Just like my desire to plant a ministry was actually a distraction, our goals and careers, while from the purest intentions, can be distractions from the calling that God actually has for our lives. Jobs can be distractions because they fulfill a need for financial stability. Sometimes financial comfort is a hindrance instead of a blessing. God could be calling one of you to quit your job and become a missionary in another country or even a minister in the city you live. If you are so focused on staying financially comfortable, though, you will miss out on a great opportunity to further the kingdom of God. We need the discernment to recognize whether God is in our career or if He is leading us elsewhere.

We need discernment to know whether things that appear to be good are from God or are actually distractions to keep us from learning to BE like Him.

EMOTIONS

Emotions can also be distractions from us truly becoming who we are called to be if we allow them to control us. Emotions are a part of us. God Himself has emotions and created us with them as well, since we are made in His image. The difference is that He rules His own emotions, whereas we cannot. Because we are corrupted by sin, our emotions and flesh will control us until they are surrendered to the Holy Spirit. Until we are sanctified and renewed by the Holy

Spirit, our natural tendencies will always seek to do what brings us pleasure and happiness. We will do whatever we can to alleviate the negative emotions we feel in order to feel better. As we follow Him, the Holy Spirit will teach us self-control as we learn to BE who He has called us to be. For instance, when we are angry, the natural response to that emotion if we let it control us is to lash out in anger. Or if we are sexually aroused, our natural response is to have sex or, in today's culture, to look at porn. The enemy knows this and will always try to distract us by putting us in situations where those emotions will be strongest. Fortunately, we have the Holy Spirit inside of us to help us discern those temptations and give us the strength to not be ruled by those emotions. We must learn to turn to Him in those instances. We must let Him be our strength instead of trying to defeat the temptation to give into our emotions on our own. This is only done through letting Him teach us to simply BE and let Him do.

STAGNATION

Another way the enemy comes in during seasons of preparation to distract us from growing is when he puts things in front of us that keep us spiritually stagnant and complacent. Stagnation is simply when we aren't doing anything to grow or help others grow. It can happen to us as individuals and corporately as the Church. Some of us aren't learning anything new about God because we've stopped studying His word. A lot of us aren't experiencing His presence because we aren't seeking Him in prayer and worship. Churches aren't seeing lives changed because of this. Stagnation stems from either a contentedness with where we are in life and not knowing that we've actually stopped growing, or from just being spiritually lazy. We're distracted by Netflix, books, video games, hanging out with friends, or whatever hobby you have. While none of these are bad things per se, they can be if we're choosing them over being with God. The enemy knows this and will use them to distract us from getting closer to God. God wants us to get to where we can discern that these distractions are actually hindering our growth and keeping us stagnant. The challenge when we recognize this is to be consistent and to manage our time well so that we don't slip back into spiritual complacency and stagnation. Sacrifices need to be made in order to achieve and experience the growth that God wants for us. The sacrifice could be to give up sleep and get up earlier to read the Bible and pray, or to not watch Netflix at night after work. Instead of doing things that don't help you achieve growth, find an alternative that would help, such as reading spiritual growth books, or going to hang out with people from your church community and have more intentional conversations about the growth process. Remove whatever is keeping you stagnant and replace it with things that will help you become who God has called you to BE.

PRACTICE MAKES PERFECT

God wants to bring us to a place in our journey with Him that we learn to BE like Jesus. He brings us through seasons of preparation where He prunes the things out of us that don't belong. During these seasons, He gives us the discernment to recognize the distractions that inhibit us from becoming more like Him. It's also during the season of preparation that mastering the spiritual disciplines or practices that God has given us can be helpful in preventing stagnation. If you're wondering what these spiritual practices or disciplines are, here are a few: prayer, reading scripture, fasting, meditating on the things of God, having a day of Sabbath, having a healthy community of fellow followers of Jesus, waiting on God, personal and corporate culture of praise and worship, and solitude. These are just a few mentioned in scripture that Jesus Himself practiced. As the saying goes, "practice makes perfect." The more you practice the spiritual disciplines, the more your spiritual discernment and hunger for more of God grows. Otherwise, you'll become complacent and remain satisfied with just enough of Him to get by.

The only way to endure a season of preparation is humility. Only when we have humility can we recognize our need for Him to change us. Humility allows us to wait on Him and serve Him through the pruning. Humility allows us to BE like Jesus.

CHAPTER 9
YOUR REALITY

As we go through the seasons of life, we see the points where the fruit of our labors shows. These are exciting times. We see this in our own natural seasons: winter turns into spring, which is the time to sow, and new life begins. Then spring turns into summer and we see that the things that we planted sprout. The new life thrives. This also is shown in our lives with Christ. As we follow Him through the hard seasons, we start to see how He transforms us.

There are opportunities for growth during each season we go through. I mentioned a few of them in the previous chapters. God uses these trials and challenges to shape us into the people He wants us to BE. However, it's up to us how we grow during these seasons.

SEEDS OF TRUTH

Picture this image in your mind.

"A farmer went out to sow his seed. As he was scattering the seed, some fell along the path, and the birds came and ate it up. Some fell on rocky places, where it had little soil. It sprang up rapidly, but when the sun came up, the plants were scorched. They withered because they had no roots. Other seeds fell among thorns, which grew up and choked the plants. Still other seeds fell on good soil, where it produced a crop—a hundred, sixty or thirty times what was sown."

Most of you might recognize this illustration as the Parable of the Sower, a parable that Jesus tells in Matthew 13.

In this passage, Jesus was talking about how different people react to the truth. He is the farmer. The seed is the truth that He sows. The ground types are people the truth is sown into. Some people's hearts are hard as a rock. They don't listen to the truth because they are so set in their beliefs and cannot produce fruit. Some people surround themselves with people who influence their beliefs. If truth seeds are planted, these influencers come and try to steal the truth to keep them from believing it. The seed of truth is not planted in them before it is stolen by society or choked out by situations. As a result, they will never grow and bear fruit. Then, there are those who are fertile soil. The seed of truth is planted deeply within them. Despite things trying to keep the seed from growing, the truth thrives, bursts forth from the ground, and produces fruit of its own.

Jesus was talking about the message of the gospel in these verses and how people responded to it. There is another lesson we can learn from them, though. God is trying to plant seeds inside of you that will grow and bear fruit. How they grow depends on what kind of ground you are during hard seasons. We still have the potential to be infertile soil or fertile soil, even if we are trying to follow Jesus. What our focus is on during the seasons He brings us through and our perspectives about what is going on in our lives determines how the truth will grow inside of us and become our reality.

FOCUS DETERMINES YOUR REALITY

What you focus on will be what you pursue. You will pursue godly things if God is your focus. You will pursue ungodly things if your focus isn't on God. This is the reason it is so important for a follower of Jesus to keep his/her focus on Jesus. Nothing can distract us from pursuing Him when our focus is on Him. There are many things in our lives today that can distract us from pursuing Him. This is especially true during hard seasons. Our emotions are all over the place. All we want is to escape the pain and stress from whatever the situation is.

There is a story in the Gospels that illustrates my point. Jesus had gone to be by Himself one day and told the disciples to cross the sea. While they were sailing, they saw Jesus walking on the water towards them, but didn't recognize Him because they thought He was a ghost. He told them to not fear, that it was Him. Peter responded that if it was Him to call him out on the water with Him. Jesus replied, "come." Peter stepped out of the boat and started walking towards Him. While this was happening, there was a storm, so after Peter began walking towards Jesus, he saw the waves and how huge they were and became afraid. He started sinking and cried out for Jesus to help Him. Jesus stretched out His hand and saved Him, saying,

"you of little faith. Why did you doubt?"

MATTHEW 14:31

There are two lessons we can learn here. I want to talk about one of them in this chapter. I'll talk about the second in the next chapter. The first lesson we can learn is that what we focus on determines our reality. If we focus on the storm, the storm becomes our reality. If we put our focus on Jesus and what He is doing in us, He becomes our reality. One is the truth, the other is a lie. Peter's focus was taken off Jesus and the truth and put on the storm. The truth was this: he could walk on water with Jesus because he was with Jesus, the creator of the universe who had power over creation itself. Peter forgot that truth for a moment, even while he was experiencing it, and believed the lie that it was stormy and he would drown. That became His reality. He started sinking, even though seconds before, his reality was that he was walking on the water with Jesus.

How many times have we experienced the power of God at work in our lives, but still put our focus on the problem instead of the solution? When this happens, the problems and challenges that we are experiencing in our hard seasons become the reality we believe in and look at. Our perspective of the situation shifts from one where we know God is bigger than the problem to one where we doubt, just like Peter. Even if we've experienced great miracles before, we still somehow get distracted by the problem.

The truth is this: God is our sustainer, protector, provider, defender, and whatever else that we need in life. He has the answer to every question we have, and He is everything we need for every situation and season. With Him, we can walk on the water in the middle of a storm. We can walk in freedom from our struggles, because He is the one who gives true, lasting freedom. When we follow Him, never getting distracted, we will take on His characteristics, or the fruit of the Spirit mentioned in Galatians. During hard seasons where we experience challenges, the reality of a follower of Jesus should be naturally responding to these challenges with the fruit of the Spirit instead of the fruit of the flesh. When we focus on Jesus and walk with Him, He empowers us to live like Him through the help of His Holy Spirit. This is our reality.

There are always other answers and things that we can turn to. However, they don't compare to Him and will always fail us. The question we have to ask ourselves is this. What is our focus on during the storms we face? Will we remember the truth and walk with Jesus on the stormy water like Peter started out doing? Or will we look to other things or even our own abilities to help us during the storm?

PERSPECTIVE SHIFTS

I want to ask this question to spark some thought. Why would you turn to things to help your situation that will always fail? Even as followers of Jesus, we sometimes have that tendency. There is a basic answer to this: our perspectives change easily. Perspective is how we view things or situations. In Star Wars, Obi Wan Kenobi says that Luke Skywalker's dad is dead. But when it is revealed that Darth Vader is Anakin Skywalker, Luke's father, Obi Wan tells Luke that what he says is true from a certain point of view. From Obi Wan's perspective, Anakin Skywalker died when he became Darth Vader. Regardless of if it was true, that was his reality. Anakin was dead. Vader was alive. Our perspectives as followers of Jesus can shift when our focus is not on God. We see the pain or storm, and our perspective shifts from one of faith in the truth to one of self-preservation.

Our perspective about a situation determines what we continue to focus on and, as a result, it becomes our reality. When we turn our attention away from God during a trial or storm, even for a brief second, our perspective about the situation can instantly change. Our reality gets distorted and we chase a lie instead of the truth. When Peter got distracted from the miracle of walking on the water with Jesus, he allowed his perspective of the situation to change. His perspective went from "if Jesus says I can do it, I can do it even in a storm" to "oh no! I'm going to drown!" Because his perspective about the situation changed, his reality changed from walking on the water with Jesus to sinking. What would have happened if his perspective didn't change? He would have put his focus back on Jesus and continued to walk with Him, even though the storm was raging around him.

The same can be true of us. The perspective you have during the hard seasons will influence what you focus on. It will become the reality you see and pursue, regardless of if it's truth. Ultimately, it will determine the fruit you produce and how you grow as a follower of Jesus. Fortunately, Jesus gives us plenty of opportunities to turn our attention back to Him if we lose focus. Peter himself remembered who he was with as he was sinking and cried out for help. He learned a valuable lesson in this moment that we can all learn as well. Jesus will never leave us and picks us up when we fall. His challenge for all of us, though, is to get to the point in our journey with Him where our perspectives don't change. Even in the storm, our perspective and focus remain on Him and the truth as we walk with Him through the storms. This can only happen if we, like Peter, continue to walk with Him, growing and learning from Him so that we can BE like Him in every situation.

ABIDING

I believe that the most important perspective that a follower of Jesus should have is that of ABIDING in Him. Jesus teaches us what it means to abide in John 15. He explains that He is the true vine and we are the branches. He wants us to bear good fruit, but the only way that a branch can bear fruit is if it remains attached to the vine. He challenges us to always abide in Him.

So how can we apply this principle of abiding when we go through hard seasons? The word abide that Jesus used in this passage means to remain. So what He is saying is "remain in me." I want to put this in my own words to describe what Jesus is saying. He is saying to us: "Be with Me. Listen to My teachings and learn what it means to be My follower. And as you are with Me and obey My teachings, let them become a part of you so that you can BE like Me."

Jesus is the source of life. He is the answer to every problem and what we need in every situation. So when we abide in Him, we are connected to Him, just like a branch that is attached to the vine. The branch is being fed and given life by the vine. Only when we are connected to Him during our hard seasons can we be given what we need to endure those trials and come out whole and perfect. If we allow ourselves to become disconnected from Him during the hard seasons, we will "wither and be cast into the fire." This means we will bring about our own self-destruction if we turn from Him when we need Him the most.

Someone who remains in Him listens to His words and abides in them. As they listen to Him, His words become part of who they are. David puts it this way in Psalm 119:11.

> *"I have hidden Your word in my heart that I may not*
> *sin against You."*

I want to put this another way to go along with this idea of developing the perspective of resting and abiding.

> *"As I have decided to follow Jesus and abide in Him,*

116

*I have listened to what He has said in His word. I
have allowed these words and the truth they hold
to penetrate so deep into my heart that they have
become part of who I am. I believe and obey His
word. As hardships come, His words and His
Spirit help me resist the temptations that come to
distract me from the truth. Even though the
season may be difficult, I am able to remember
these words and abide in Him through the
season."*

This is what I believe every follower of Jesus should focus on in every season. I want to challenge you to pray this over yourself every day and let these words become your reality.

As this becomes your reality, you will start to BE more and more like Jesus. There are two characteristics of Jesus that every follower should have as they go through hard seasons. They know how to rest and they realize that life is not about them.

Rest and be Glad

When I think about what it means for me to rest, I picture myself stretched out in a hammock at the Great Lake I live close to, Lake Erie. I also picture myself in the fall, sitting outside by a campfire on a chilly day, with a guitar in my hands. These are my happy places where I am best able to think the clearest and focus only on God. While in these places, it's easy to rest in His presence and hear His voice without the distractions of life. I'm sure each of you reading this has your own happy place as well. A place where you can just be at peace and feel God's presence the most.

Another scenario that I thought of as I'm writing this that shows what resting looks like is a nation celebrating after winning a war. They have now entered a period where soldiers can go home to their families and enjoy the peace that they have fought for. Instead of fighting and killing, they can learn to smile and laugh again. They can watch their kids grow and enjoy spending time with them. They can do whatever makes them happy without having the fear that comes with war.

I also picture college students who are celebrating the beginning of winter or summer break after a hard finals week. After a semester of studying, doing homework, preparing presentations, writing essays, or freaking out because they waited until the last minute to study for the test or write the essay they have due the next day because they were too busy partying, they can now enjoy the summer. (Yes, I made this a very long run-on sentence intentionally.) They can now enjoy the break vacationing with their families, going to weddings, working at their jobs to make money, or even staying at home and playing video games. No more tests. No more presentations. No more essays. No more stress. They can now focus on doing whatever allows them to rest and be happy.

These moments might seem perfect. We all strive to experience them. However, we also know that these moments never seem to last, especially when life is hard and you are suffering. Some of us perhaps feel like this will never happen to us because we just can't seem to rest. We feel like we are so busy or it seems like our lives are just too hard and depressing. However, I don't believe that it is God's plan to leave us feeling helpless in suffering. I believe God wants to bring us to a point in our relationship with Him that resting in Him is normal. A relationship with God that is so deep that nothing can faze us. We know He is with us and that He is everything we need and we can rest in that truth.

A perfect example of someone who has learned to rest in God is Jesus Himself. There is a story in the Gospels that illustrates this. One day, He and the disciples were sailing across the Sea of Galilee in the middle of a fierce storm. Jesus had fallen asleep in the boat while the disciples were trying to keep them afloat. They woke Him up and asked Him if he cared if they drowned. His response was to speak to the storm and command it to be still. It immediately obeyed, and the disciples were astounded.

Jesus had such a relationship with the Father that He emulated rest. He was so completely at peace emotionally and mentally that during a fierce storm, He slept through it. This is a perfect picture of what our emotional and mental state during the storms of life could look like if we learned to rest in perfect peace.

Some of you might be skeptical about this, which is understandable. As you read this, you might be thinking, "I'm not Jesus, I'm human! It's impossible for me to be completely at peace all the time!" Maybe you struggle with depression or anxiety. You might have attention deficit disorder, which makes you feel chaotic all the time. You might live a busy life. Some of you might be in the middle of one of the seasons I mentioned in the past few chapters and be experiencing pain and lots of stress for whatever reason. In these situations, it's hard to rest. I get it. I find it so hard to rest sometimes myself. Just today as I was driving, I got behind several slow drivers who caused my impatience to well up. I'll be honest, I just about started yelling and blowing my horn at them. I thought about this section and started laughing at the absurdity. Here I am writing about resting and having peace, but I'm not resting in Him in traffic.

Let me just say that it's ok. We're all a work in progress. It's a one step at a time kind of journey. We all go through days where we "get up on the wrong side of the bed." We all experience emotions we have to learn to control with the help of the Holy Spirit. However, it doesn't change the fact that perfect peace is a promise from God Himself. Once He promises something, He always fulfills it. He promises in Isaiah 26:3 that He will

> *"keep him in perfect peace, whose mind is stayed on*
> *You, because he trusts in You."*

Having perfect peace doesn't mean that you won't have emotions, though. God Himself has emotions and created us to have emotions. Jesus got angry and sad several times in the Gospels. Having perfect peace in times of storms means we are not ruled by the emotions that come with it. When you learn to rest in His peace, the decisions you make while you experience those emotions will be based on the truth, not on what you feel at the moment.

Something else that I want to mention too is that learning to rest not only comes with perfect peace, but with perfect joy. When we learn to rest in Him, we gain an understanding of what the purpose of trials is: to perfect us. James says in James 1 to

> *"count it all joy when you fall into various trials,*
> *knowing that the testing of your faith produces*
> *patience. But let patience have its perfect work,*
> *that you may be perfect and complete, lacking*
> *nothing."*

When we learn to rest in God, we are able to see that God is planting seeds inside of us. He's using trials to grow us and bring us to perfection and completion. Once we have this understanding and perspective, we learn to "count it all joy when we fall into various trials." Joy here is translated as to be glad. So what this is saying is that we welcome trials. We are glad to go through them, knowing that God is using them to make us into the perfect, spotless people He has called us to BE. We don't have to DO anything other than follow Him through the hard seasons, knowing that He is the one that will do the work for us as we rest in Him.

IT'S NOT ABOUT ME

The second perspective that I believe every follower of Jesus should have is that life is not about us. God is not bringing us through the trials only for our own benefit, but for His glory. He uses those situations to make Himself known to those around us. Yes, we will definitely benefit, but we are not called to keep what we have learned and gained to ourselves. There are others going through the same seasons that don't know God or don't understand how God wants them to grow. God brings us through the hard seasons in order to grow His Kingdom.

- *Revival*

Something that we see throughout history is that the greatest revivals came after God's people endured a hard season. We hear about revivals happening, such as the Welsh Revival, the Great Awakenings, the Azusa Street revival, and others. Each of these revivals occurred after seasons of change, preparation, and waiting. They held prayer meetings on university campuses or in homes where they would pray for months for God to move. After months of persevering and enduring ridicule from people, God honored their prayers and obedience and moved in powerful ways. Thousands of people became followers of Jesus. People came from all over the world to experience what was happening in the locations these revivals started. Evangelists such as Charles and John Wesley, the founders of the Methodist denomination, left their homes in order to bring the gospel to the nations. Missions movements were birthed from these revivals. During these revivals, God would use people to perform miracles, signs and wonders, showing His power to the lost in order to bring more to Him. We are still living in the legacy and seeing the fruit that grew during these revivals.

In Scripture, we see this occur on the Day of Pentecost. Jesus had commanded His disciples to wait in the upper room for the gift of the Holy Spirit. According to Acts 2, they waited day after day, praying. Then, on the Day of Pentecost, God fulfilled His promise and sent the Holy Spirit, filling them with the power to be better witnesses, as Jesus promised. That day began the disciples' season of fulfillment where what they were waiting for happened, just like Jesus said it would. 3000 people were saved on that day, and the church was born.

If we are to see a move of the Holy Spirit occur today that will spark an even greater revival than the ones I've mentioned, we must learn to keep our focus on Jesus through the hard seasons of preparation and change He wants to bring us through.

- *Blessing*

Something else that I see throughout scripture is that when the trials the heroes of the faith have to endure have ended, God blesses them. Joseph became the second most powerful person in the world after a season where he suffered as a slave and was imprisoned because of his brothers' jealousy. Job endured the hardship of suffering, focusing on the truth even when he lost everything. In the end, his wealth and family were doubled after this season ended. The nation of Israel suffered at the hand of the Egyptians for generations until God delivered them into their promised land. There are countless other stories in scripture of God's grace and mercy being shown when He gives His people blessing after they endure hardship. Many of us today can think of times where God has provided for our needs, or healed us, or delivered us from our own sin and stupidity.

However, like I've said earlier in this section, God never brings us out of hard situations into His blessings only for our benefit. He brings us through them to bless the world and people around us. Joseph was raised up and blessed with riches and position, not so that he could benefit from it, but to save the entire world from starvation during the famine. His own family benefited from the favor of God that was with Joseph. The nation of Israel was saved from slavery and brought into the Promised Land so that God could honor the covenant He had made with their ancestor Abraham. He had promised Abraham that He would bless him as he followed where He led. He also promised He would make his descendants a great nation so that they could be a blessing to the entire world. Israel went through many trials and struggles. Even with all of those hard seasons, though, we see that out of Israel came the greatest Blessing that God could ever give to humanity: Jesus Himself. Israel is still blessing the world because of God's blessing and promise to Abraham.

FOR HIS KINGDOM

Growing His kingdom is the most important reason we have to persevere during times of hardships and seasons of preparation and waiting. God does not bring us through these trials into growth and blessing for our own benefit but to grow His Kingdom. Lives would not have been changed if the leaders of the revivals I mentioned hadn't endured their hardships. If the fathers of our faith had not endured their suffering for the sake of the gospel, we would not live in the freedom that we have. The gospel would never have come to the Gentiles. Their suffering led to our freedom. A lot of us today are a part of the legacy that stemmed from the sacrifice of the church fathers and from the revivals they led. We would not be here if they had not had their focus on Jesus.

I would encourage and challenge those of you who are in your season of preparation with this thought. There are lost souls who are depending on you to endure so that you can see His kingdom come. Keep going and pressing on. Stay focused on Him and on the goal of growing His kingdom. Give everything you have and surrender everything you are to see His will be done on earth as it is in heaven. Never lose the perspective that you must rest in Him. This is the only way to find perfect peace and joy in Him as you go through the hard seasons. Rest in him to keep from getting distracted by anything the enemy and your flesh will throw at you to give up and lose your focus. There are people depending on you to endure so that they can experience the rest, peace, joy, and hope that you experience. Run the race set before you with joy, even though it will be very hard. Celebrate the victories that God has won for you. Get up when you stumble and take His hand again. The joy we have in Him and hope of perfection are worth the pain and suffering.

THE SOIL OF YOUR LIFE

I want to end this chapter by asking this question again, "What kind of ground are you?" At the beginning of this chapter, I talked about the Parable of the Sower. I mentioned God wants to sow seeds in you that will produce a great harvest. Your growth depends on what kind of soil you are. As I finish this section, I want to reiterate this. Even as followers of Jesus, we have the potential to be infertile ground or fertile ground. Even followers of Jesus who have lived their whole lives following can be susceptible to the lies of the enemy who is trying to keep us from growing. Our hearts could be hardened to the seeds of truth that God is sowing by our own pride and self-deception. I have experienced this myself, and I'm sure you have too. I've seen many people going through a hard time saying that "the devil was attacking" them. In reality, they were in a season of preparation, but were not learning the lesson God was trying to teach them. This was me at one point, as I talked about in the last chapter. I believed that all the trouble that I experienced was just distractions by the enemy to get me off the path. I didn't recognize that I was hindering my personal growth. When I recognized that and allowed my heart to become softened, it was like a breath of fresh air. That's when I could see that God was leading me in a new direction and teaching me to let go of my will. It was at this point that I saw what He was doing and I experienced a new level of growth in my journey learning to BE like Jesus.

Sometimes the seeds that God is sowing can still be stolen before they are planted or choked out by the teachings and patterns of the society we live in. Here's a good example. I've seen people who were sick and had people pray for them for healing many times. When they never got healed, they were told that God didn't heal them because they "didn't have faith." They believed this lie. God wanted to plant a seed of the truth inside of them. He wanted them to know that He loved them and cared for their situation, even if it might not seem like it. Unfortunately, that seed could never be planted. It was stolen by a lie told by someone professing to be a follower of Jesus, causing them even more pain. They never developed a healthy perspective or relationship with Jesus and, as a result, never learned to rest in God, experiencing His peace and joy. How many people are unable to gain a healthy perspective of God and suffering because of false teaching? How many false teachings do we believe that, unknowingly, cause our hearts to be infertile ground during hard seasons?

God wants to plant seeds in His church today that grow into huge trees that provide shelter and fruit for the entire world. When these seeds of truth can't grow, we can't gain the perspectives that I've mentioned throughout this chapter. As a result, our focus cannot stay on Christ through our hard seasons. But when we allow ourselves to stay humble as we follow Jesus, our hearts will be fertile. All it takes is a life totally surrendered to Jesus. We must remember that we don't have to DO anything other than just simply BE His obedient, humble follower. It's through following Him that we learn to allow the seeds He is sowing to be planted in us. Even in our hard seasons, we can learn to rest and be glad in order to keep our focus firmly on Him.

CHAPTER 10
THE GOSPEL OF TRUTH

f there is one thing I want to emphasize in this book, it's that Jesus came to bring mankind out of captivity to sin and death into freedom and new life. This is the gospel of truth. This is the only way for us to BE who He has called us to BE. There are many "truths" out there for us to believe in, but they all eventually lead to self destruction. There is one truth that stands above them all and it's this: Jesus is "the way, truth, and life" according to John 14:6. This truth has stood the test of time and is the hope for all mankind.

FROM SLAVES TO SONS

The truth is, before we become followers of Jesus, we are slaves to our own sin nature. We didn't start out that way though. In the beginning, God created Adam and Eve in His image, perfect and pure. They were the ultimate creation, the ones into whom God had breathed His breath, the very essence of who He is, giving them life. He gave them authority over all the earth, telling them to take dominion over it. However, they gave up this authority to Satan when they disobeyed God's command to not eat the forbidden fruit. Because sin cannot exist in the presence of God, the consequence of their choice was mankind's separation from God and death. However, God had a plan. A plan that would demonstrate His grace and mercy and make it so mankind would not have to DO anything other than believe to gain back their freedom and life with Him.

Fast forward a few hundred years and we see God establish a covenant with His chosen people, Israel. He gave them the law that we see in Leviticus and Deuteronomy, establishing a system that would allow them to atone for their sins each year. A sacrifice would be made of an animal, usually a pure, spotless lamb, to take on the sins of the entire nation for the year. This animal would take their punishment for them. While this worked to reestablish a relationship with God to some extent, it could not completely redeem mankind for all eternity. We were still separated from knowing God fully. God knew this, though. His plan since the fall included the answer. Humanity needed some help from God Himself. The law was meant to show us that. Only He was perfect enough to be the pure, spotless sacrifice that would completely atone for the punishment we deserved because of sin.

A few hundred years after Israel's captivity in Babylon, the result of their rebellion, and their eventual return, we see something happen that would change things forever. God Himself became a man in the form of Jesus, lived a perfect life, and then died in order to fulfill every requirement for our eternal redemption. We didn't have to DO a thing. He did it for us.

That wasn't the end, though. He came back to life after three days, demonstrating His power over death. Because of this, not only is our debt of eternal punishment paid for, but we can have new life in Him if we choose to follow Him. New life means living in freedom from what kept us bound for so long. We have the opportunity to

BE a different person, to BE like Him in every way. We have the opportunity to go from being slaves to being His sons and daughters. This is the truth of the gospel.

The thing about His grace and love, though, is that it has to be received for it to take effect. We have the choice whether to take the freedom that He wants to give us or to reject it in favor of DOING our own thing. Living a life of freedom requires us to die to the old ways of doing things and follow Jesus in every way. Yes, it's hard. As I've mentioned in previous chapters of this book, we will face trials and have to endure pain during the seasons God leads us through. What we gain as we become who God wants us to be is worth the pain we go through during the growth process.

THE NATURE OF CHRIST

The truth of the gospel is that not only do we gain salvation when we choose to follow Christ, we also gain the grace and power we need to live exactly as God wants us to while we are still alive. As we abide in Him, as He teaches us in John 15, He reveals Himself to us. He helps us understand the truth of who He is. As we develop a relationship with Him, our love for Him grows. As we spend time with Him, we start to take on His nature with the help and empowerment of the Holy Spirit. We will see the fruit of the Spirit that I've mentioned in an earlier chapter start to grow in our lives. These fruits are characteristics of God Himself. He is the author and perfect representation of love, joy, peace, patience, kindness, goodness, faithfulness, gentleness, and self-control. As we learn to BE His followers and let Him do the work in us, we will start to manifest these traits as well. Like I said in an earlier chapter, where before your natural fleshly tendency was to live in hate, anger, selfish desires, lust, etc., you will now be able to resist those temptations, seeing the truth, and living like Christ. Where before you felt like giving up during the hard season, you are able to clearly see the truth and it helps you endure. God wants to not only use those hard situations to grow and bless you, but to also build His kingdom and show His glory as He leads you through the trials. Because you understand this truth, you can endure those trials joyfully, just like Christ endured the cross joyfully for us, knowing that the trials and suffering would lead to the promised salvation and perfection and Kingdom expansion.

THERE IS MORE

One final thought that I want to leave you with in this last chapter as I finish this book is this: there is more. He has created each of us to BE His followers. As we follow and obey Him, He wants us to become like Him in every way. Here's the thing that a lot of followers of Jesus have forgotten. Jesus was not only a perfect man who wants us to be perfect, just like Him, He was also a man of action. He healed the sick, raised the dead, turned water into wine, walked on water, and cast out demons. He wants us to do the same things He did too and more. His command to us is to go preach the gospel to all people and make disciples. It wasn't a suggestion. All it takes is for us to have the faith to obey. He wants us to BE people of action who live out the gospel in faith and see Him move in the way He wants to.

I mentioned in the last chapter that the story of Peter walking on water had two lessons we could learn from. The first was that our focus determines our reality. If our focus is on Jesus, we will BE like Him even through the storms. The second is this. Peter was the only disciple out of the twelve who had the faith to get out of the boat. The others just assumed they couldn't do it. How many of us never even think to step out in faith just because we assume we can't do what Jesus does? I want to make this challenge for all of us as followers of Jesus. Our mentality about what our potential is as followers of Jesus has to align with Scripture. This is the seed that God wants to plant inside of us that the enemy wants to steal. Paul tells us in Philippians 4:13 that

> *"I can do all things through Christ who strengthens me."*

This verse applies to all of us, not just Paul. We can do anything in the power of Jesus. Jesus Himself tells us we will do all that He did and even greater things if we follow Him. If He tells us to do something, we can do it. That is His promise to us. Paul emphasizes this in 2 Timothy 3:16-17 saying that

> *"all Scripture is given by inspiration of God, and is profitable for doctrine, for reproof, for correction, for instruction in righteousness, that the man of God may be complete, thoroughly equipped for every good work."*

Paul was telling Timothy that we are equipped with everything we need to grow the Kingdom, just like Jesus.

You may say, "doesn't this contradict what you're saying in this book? I thought we didn't have to DO anything to BE like Jesus." I want to remind you, though, that what I mean by this is that we don't have to do anything in our own power. He does the work while we BE His obedient followers. We don't save people, He does. We don't heal, He does. All we have to do is just take the step out of the boat with Him when He tells us to and go to the people He loves and wants to set free. Just like Jesus.

EQUIPPED

We all have a purpose and a calling. That purpose is first and foremost to BE like Him. Throughout this book, I've talked about how He makes us more like Him by bringing us through seasons of growth and teaching us how to listen to and obey His voice. But how does He equip us to BE more like Him to grow His kingdom? Let me answer this question with two questions. "What are your passions that drive you?" "What are your talents?"

NATURAL GIFTS

The reason I asked these questions is this. The passions that we have drive us to accomplish a goal. Some people have a passion for exercise. That passion pushes them to grow their ability to exercise. I personally couldn't care less about exercise, but I have a passion for music. These passions change and grow over time as we follow Christ. When we learn to BE like Him, He instills His passions inside of us. His heart is for the lost. As we progress in our journey to BE like Him, He puts a passion to reach the lost inside of us as well. He then equips us with talents that give us the ability to achieve this purpose to see the lost found and grow His kingdom. These natural talents are part of who you are. I'll use my passion for music as an example. God has taken my passion for music and grown it into a passion to use music to glorify Him. I wasn't always talented at music. However, when He called me to be a worship leader, He started developing my musical ability. Twenty years of experience later, I can now play drums, guitar, piano and can sing. He gave me a passion to see people enter His presence and equipped me with the talent to fulfill the purpose He had for my life. As I have been obedient in that calling, that talent has grown. The passion has grown as well. I love seeing people encounter Him and their lives be changed as I lead them into His presence through music. There is no greater calling than to use my giftings to build His kingdom and see lives be changed.

There have been some people who, when asked what their passions and talents are, respond, "I don't know." They didn't know what they were passionate about or what their giftings were. Some of you who are reading this might fit this description. I want to challenge you to figure this out if you want to learn to BE more like Christ. I would also encourage you to not overthink it. Some of you might have natural giftings that you might not be aware of. We, as a society, tend to elevate certain talents above others. No gift is more important than another. We all have our part to play in the Kingdom of God. Figure out what drives you and what your talents are and use them to grow His kingdom. Let me give you an example from scripture. Paul gave the same challenge to the people of Romans in Romans 12:4-8.

> *"For as we have many members in one body, but all the members do not have the same function, so we, being many, are one body in Christ, and individually members of one another. Having then gifts differing according to the grace that is given to us, let us use them: if prophecy, let us prophecy in proportion to our faith; or ministry, let us use it in our ministering; he who teaches, in teaching; he who exhorts, in exhortation; he who gives, with liberality; he who leads, with diligence; he who shows mercy, with cheerfulness."*

BUILD HIS KINGDOM

Think about what Paul is saying. We are members of a body. Just like each part of our natural body has a purpose, we each have a purpose that God has created us to perform to help the body function properly. If we aren't performing that purpose, the body stops functioning properly. Paul lists a few giftings to emphasize this. Some of you might have one of these giftings and not even realize it. Teachers should teach, givers should give, encouragers should encourage, prophets should prophecy, etc. I'll add a few to this list. People who love babies or children should be in the nursery or children's ministry. Someone who loves landscaping and is good at it should use that talent and passion to grow the kingdom. Someone who is a plumber should plumb toilets for the Kingdom of God. Knowledge about something is a gift that God wants to use to grow His kingdom. Someone who is a doctor should realize that their knowledge of medicine is given to them by God to heal people. A lawyer or politician should use their knowledge of the law to grow the Kingdom. Here's an overlooked one. If you're gifted with your own children, raise them up well to be followers of Jesus. Parenting is a gift given by God to grow His kingdom. We need to view it as such. The list can go on and on. There are lots of talents out there. Find yours and use it to grow His Kingdom.

In fact, every ability that we have is a gift and talent given to us by God to grow His kingdom. All of us breathe. Here's an idea for you to think about. Your breath is a gift from God that can be used to grow His kingdom. Our natural ability to move our fingers is a gift from God that can be used in some way. Your ability to smile is a gift from God to be used. You just have to figure out how you can use these abilities to help build His Kingdom. Get creative. Paul says in 1 Corinthians 10 that everything we do, we do for the glory of God. He's talking about what things are lawful and unlawful to do as Christians in this passage, but it still applies to this principle. We are meant to use whatever abilities we have been given by God for His glory and to grow His kingdom.

SUPERNATURAL GIFTS

Something that I love about this journey with Christ is that it's a partnership with Him. We walk with Him; He does the work through us. He does this by giving us giftings. I've mentioned natural ones already that are part of who you are. There are other gifts, though, that He gives us to be better witnesses for Him. These are called the gifts of the Spirit mentioned in 1 Corinthians 12. I've mentioned some of these gifts in earlier chapters. These gifts are supernaturally given, meaning that the Holy Spirit gives these gifts to us supernaturally. They are not a natural part of us. We cannot use these gifts on our own. The ability to use them comes from learning to BE His follower. We develop the ability to listen to His voice and obey as we follow Him. As I mentioned in chapter 3, the gifts of prophecy, word of knowledge, word of wisdom, tongues, and interpretation of tongues are Him speaking through us. The gifts are meant to encourage and build the church. As He leads us, we also see two other gifts in operation through us: healing and working of miracles. They are demonstrations of His power through us. The gifts of faith and discernment of spirits are given to us to help us grow as we learn to BE like Him. I will talk more about these giftings in my next book *You BE You.*

DON'T SETTLE

As I've said throughout this entire book, God has a plan. It's a plan for us to BE whole. He set this plan into motion by sending Jesus to redeem us and bring us back into relationship with Him. We don't have to DO anything to achieve this perfection other than BE His followers. As we follow Him, abiding in Him, He makes us more like Jesus in every way. This is the calling. This is our goal. To BE like Jesus. He does the work in and through us as we follow Him. He has also gifted us with natural and supernatural giftings to help us achieve this goal and to grow His kingdom. The problem is we have settled for just being like Jesus halfway and have either not accepted the gifts He wants to give or have neglected our talents to the point where we aren't using them. There is more that God wants to do in us and through us in order to grow His kingdom and we have to BE people of action just like Jesus was. This is the only way that we can fully BE His followers and live life with Him.

AFTERWORD

Thanks for reading my first book. For the past few years, The Holy Spirit has been leading me on this journey of learning to simply BE His follower. I am so thankful that I was able to share this journey with you. I hope that you were encouraged and inspired to join me on this journey.

Something I will let you guys in on is that the last chapter of this book is actually a preview of another book that I will release in 2023. I will continue teaching where I left off in the last chapter about being people of action, practicing being His follower, growing in our giftings, and using them to grow the Kingdom of God. I am also releasing journals in the coming months and work-books for small groups and Sunday school classes next year as well. If you enjoyed this book and felt challenged, I would encourage you to buy the sequel, journals, and the workbooks that come with both of them.

Also, if you are interested in scheduling me for a speaking event (either live or through video conferencing) at your church or confer-ence, small group/bible study, want to find out more about me, or to contact me with any comments, questions or concerns about the book, you can go to my website bentonjward.com to find ways to contact me. I would love to get to know my readers and am looking forward to hearing from you. You can also sign up for my news-letter there as well. Also if you loved the book, please leave a review.

Until then, I will leave you guys with the words of Paul as a blessing.

> *"That the eyes of your understanding being enlight-ened; that you may know what is the hope of His calling, what are the riches of the glory of His inheritance in the saints, and what is the exceeding greatness of His power toward us who believe, according to the working of His mighty power which He worked in Christ when He raised Him from the dead and seated Him at His right hand in the heavenly places, far above all principality and power and might and dominion, and every name that is named, not only in this age but also in that which is to come."*

> EPHESIANS 1: 18-21

Amen.

ABOUT THE AUTHOR

 A licensed minister with the Assemblies of God, worship leader, and life coach, Benton Ward has a passion for discipleship and to help people thrive in every area of their lives. He loves to use his talents in writing, speaking, and leading worship to help others encounter God in a life changing way. He has served as a missionary with Chi Alpha Campus Ministries, as well as a worship pastor, young adults pastor, and youth pastor. He currently resides with his wife, Megan, in Edinboro, Pennsylvania. When he is not writing, he is hanging out with his friends, playing games, with his wife eating ice cream, napping, reading, playing music, or watching Netflix. To contact Benton for speaking engagements, coaching/counseling sessions, etc, and and to subscribe to his newsletter updates visit bentonjward.com.

facebook.com/BentonJWard

instagram.com/bentonjwardauthor